A Brief Outline of Things to Come

Compiled by

THEODORE H. EPP

Author of *Nuggets from Genesis* and
Adventuring by Faith
Director of Back to the Bible Broadcast

MOODY PRESS
CHICAGO

Printed in the United States of America

FOREWORD

PROPHECY is given by God to foretell future events. Throughout the Scriptures, written over a period of 1600 years, the Holy Spirit has revealed one co-ordinative plan of the future. Jesus told His disciples that one of the reasons for prophesying was that when an event which He had foretold occurred, they would believe that He was the Son of God. Peter further enlightens us by telling us that prophecy is "a light that shineth in a dark place, until the day dawn, and the day star arise in your hearts" (II Peter 1:19).

Often prophetic subjects have become the theme of speculation. In speculating men have gone far beyond the purpose of prophetic Scriptures. I believe that the most helpful way to study prophecy is outlined for us in Revelation 1:3: "Blessed is he that readeth, and they that hear the words of this prophecy, and keep those things which are written therein: for the time is at hand." Three distinct steps are mentioned: first, *read;* second, *give heed;* third, *remember.* Nothing is said about speculating or prophesying.

This book is by no means an exhaustive study of the great prophetic subjects. Rather, it presents a brief outline of things to come. It should serve as a light in a dark place for those who believe and as a definite warning to those who have thus far rejected Christ as Saviour. It should move the Christian to take action for His Lord and should move the unsaved to accept Christ as their Saviour. "Knowing the time, that now it is high time to awake out of sleep: for now is our salvation nearer than when we believed. The night is far spent, the day is at hand: let us therefore cast off the works of darkness, and let us put on the armor of light" (Rom. 13:11, 12).

—THEODORE H. EPP

We have also a more sure word of prophecy; whereunto ye do well that ye take heed, as unto a light that shineth in a dark place, until the day dawn, and the day star arise in your hearts.

—II Peter 1:19

CONTENTS

Used by permission of Mrs. E. J. Pace, Orlando, Fla.

A BRIEF SUMMARY OF WHAT
WE MAY EXPECT

Keith L. Brooks

FULFILLED PROPHECY is conclusive evidence of the divine inspiration of the Bible.

> Remember the former things of old: for I am God, and there is none else; I am God, and there is none like me, declaring the end from the beginning, and from ancient times the things that are not yet done, saying, My counsel shall stand, and I will do all my pleasure (Isa. 46:9, 10).

None of the sacred books of other religions have in them a prophetic element. The reason is not hard to find. Had the authors attempted to foretell future events, they would have left behind them the strongest evidences of their deception. The God of the Bible alone grasps the ages. God's Book alone is largely made up of prophecy, and none can deny that the march of the ages has corroborated His prophetic statements.

These prophecies are so detailed and so specific, and they were recorded so long before the events transpired that they cannot be accounted for on the basis of human foresight. Thousands of volumes have been written throughout the Christian centuries showing how Bible predictions have passed literally into history.

The apostle Peter wrote, "The prophecy came not in old time by the will of man: but holy men of God spake as they were moved by the Holy Ghost" (II Peter 1:21).

9

"We have also a more sure word of prophecy; whereunto ye do well that ye take heed, as unto a light that shineth in a dark place, until the day dawn, and the day star arise in your hearts" (II Peter 1:19).

Herewith we set forth a few of the prophecies having to do with the consummation of the age in which we are living. As you read them and compare them with the events of which our daily papers are full, recall the challenging question put by our Lord to the religious leaders of His day: "Can ye not discern the signs of the times?" (Matt. 16:3).

INTERNATIONAL CONDITIONS PRECEDING CHRIST'S SECOND COMING

Constant rumors of war (Matt. 24:6).

Increasing world conflicts accompanied by pestilence and famine (Matt. 24:7; Isa. 13:4, 5).

Economic perils such as the nations have never known (Matt. 24:21, 22; Mark 13:19; Dan. 12:1).

The people impotent to help themselves (Ezek. 7:17, 18).

Gold and silver valueless as exchange (Ezek. 7:19).

Disastrous earthquakes (Matt. 24:7).

Increasing commotions within nations (Luke 21:9).

Fearful sights and great signs (Luke 21:11, 25).

People's hearts failing for fear (Luke 21:26; Isa. 24:17, 18).

Perilous conditions in general (II Tim. 3:1-5).

Collapse of great fortunes (James 5:1-8).

Nations utterly broken down (Isa. 24:19, 20; 51:6).

Days of darkness and gloominess (Joel 2:2).

Hellish war devices (Joel 2:3-5).

World empire attained; its final destruction (Dan. 2:40-45).

Many traitors, "fifth columnists" (Mark 13:12; Luke 21:16; II Tim. 3:3, 4).

National revival of Israel (Mark 13:28).

Russia and Germany, as one, eventually attempt to grab riches of Palestine (Ezek. 38, 39).

Increasing persecution of Christians and Jews (Dan. 7:21, 22; Jer. 30:7, 13-16; Matt. 24:9; Mark 13:13).

Final rise of an anti-God world dictator demanding allegiance of all (Dan. 7:24-26; Rev. 13:1-18); honors the god of forces (Dan. 11:36-39); overthrows many nations (Dan: 11:41, 42).

Wastes of Palestine cultivated after many cenuries of barrenness (Isa. 43:19, 20; Ezek. 34:26, 27; 36:4-10, 30, 34, 35).

Hebrew language revived after being long dead (Zeph. 3:9).

Jews return to Palestine in large numbers (Isa. 43:5, 6; 49:19; Jer. 23:3; 30:3; Ezek. 11:17, 18; Hos. 3:4, 5).

Seven years of consummation—the Great Tribulation—time of awful trouble for the Jews (Jer. 30:7; Dan. 9:27).

Religious Conditions Preceding Christ's Second Coming

Organized atheism mocks religion (Jude 18).

Rulers take counsel against God (Ps. 2:2, 3).

True religion waning, iniquity abounding (Matt. 24:12, 38).

General apostasy in Christendom (II Thess. 3:3).

Increase of spiritualistic practices (I Tim. 4:1-3).

Religion largely a matter of form (II Tim. 3:5; Rev. 3:16, 17).

Many will not endure sound doctrine (II Tim. 4:3, 4).

Damnable heresies spring up overnight (II Peter 2:1-3).

Religious fakers work seeming miracles (Mark 13:22).

Preachers ridicule the teaching of Christ's second coming (II Peter 3:3, 4).

A great world religious federation takes shape, headed by a false prophet of great power (Matt. 24:5, 11, 24; Rev. 13:11-18).

A great religious war is headed by the Beast with Palestine as the cockpit (Zech. 14:1-3; 12:2, 3; Rev. 16:16; 19:11-21).

Jew-hatred once and for all judged (Isa. 49:26; 60:14; Jer. 30:16, 17).

The Climax

In the midnight hour of the age the Lord Jesus Christ comes first for His own (Matt. 25:6).

Every eye shall see Him (Rev. 1:7).

Christ in Person (John 14:3; Acts 1:11; I Thess. 4:13-18).

Sleeping saints are raised; living believers are translated to meet Christ in the air (I Cor. 15:51-54; Phil. 3:21; John 5:24-29; I Thess. 4:15-17).

The Great Tribulation followed by His glorious coming (Matt. 24:29, 30).

The Beast Empire destroyed (Dan. 2:45).

Throne of latter-day dictators wiped out (Dan. 7:9-18).

All evil forces removed (II Thess. 1:7-10; Matt. 13:41).

All wickedness punished; righteous rule established (Ps. 98:8, 9; Isa. 2:4-22; 13:11, 12; 24:21; 26:20, 21).

Peace restored to the Holy Land, the homeland of Israel (Isa. 60:15-22; 62:1-10; Jer. 31:4-13; 33:7-18; Ezek. 34:12-14, 23-28).

The Jews worship the King of kings (Ezek. 36:22-38; 37:21-28; Hos. 14:4-9; Zech. 12:10-12).

Christ's glorious and universal reign (Ps. 47:5-9; 72:1-17; Isa. 11:1-12; 25:8, 9; 35:1-10; 65:17-25; Micah 4:1-8; Zech. 2:10-13; 14:20, 21; Rev. 21:1-7).

THE RESTORATION OF PALESTINE

M. R. DeHaan

For, behold, in those days, and in that time, when I shall bring again the captivity of Judah and Jerusalem, I will also gather all nations, and will bring them down into the valley of Jehoshaphat, and will plead with them there for my people and for my heritage Israel, whom they have scattered among the nations, and parted my land (Joel 3:1, 2).

THE LAND OF PALESTINE, about which there is so much difference of opinion today, was given by an everlasting covenant to the twelve tribes of Israel. Because of their disobedience they have been out of the land and scattered among the nations for many centuries; but they are soon again to be restored, according to the promise of God. These lands have lain practically in waste for two millenniums, but recent years have seen a tremendous revival of interest in the return of Israel to Palestine. Millions and millions of dollars have been invested in the development of the incalculable, fantastic natural resources of the land. Thousands of the seed of Jacob have immigrated to Palestine, having been driven by persecution from other countries, until now the very flower of Jewish culture is there.

Agriculturally the land of Palestine has seen the greatest boom of all time. Thousands of acres of land have been brought under cultivation. Irrigation projects running into millions of dollars have been started, and scientific agricultural methods are causing the land to produce some of the finest and choicest fruits in all the world. Surely the "dry bones" are coming together again.

In the last few years Palestine has also become the home of culture, education, and intellect. The Hebrew University on Mt. Scopus, near Jerusalem, has on its faculty men with some of the brightest, keenest minds in all the world. The famous professors who are teaching in this university are largely refugees from other European lands. This university today has more than one thousand students. Among them are one hundred American Jews who are studying there at the expense of the G.I. Bill of Rights.

In recent years the Zionist movement, organized as a world-wide attempt of Jewry, led by some of its ablest minds, has fostered the setting aside of Palestine as a home for the nation of Israel. As a result of this there is in the land of Palestine today a vigorous, growing nation of several million Jews. Diplomatic recognition has been won, the land is being reclaimed, industry is being established, and international trade is being carried on. Israel has been reborn. As a result of this the Israelite nation has been revived.

Toward the close of World War I certain events took place which made many earnest Christian students believe that the time of Israel's restoration, the setting up of the kingdom, and the return of the Messiah was very near. The Allies took Palestine, and General Allenby marched into the city and delivered it from the domination of those who had held it for many centuries. It was then that a modest little Jewish chemist made a wonderful offer to the leaders of Great Britain. At an hour of apparent defeat for the Allies this Jewish scientist, Dr. Chaim Weizmann, who is now[1] president of Palestine, introduced a formula for the most powerful explosive ever

[1] 1950.

discovered up to that time—TNT. He donated the discovery to his beloved country, Britain. That was the one event which did more to turn the tide of victory for the Allies than anything else. This is a matter of history, and it may be corroborated by reference to an encyclopedia.

Then Lord Balfour announced that in the event of victory over the enemy the land of Palestine would be given to the nation of Israel as their national home—the dream of Zionism. The war did end as a result of the contribution of this Jewish chemist, Dr. Weizmann, and the Balfour Declaration gave Britain the mandate over the land of Palestine. Here, we believe, was Britain's golden opportunity. She had it in her power to clear the land of its unlawful possessors and make it exclusively the home of God's scattered people. All Christendom believed that the time for the restoration had come.

However, for reasons of expediency or otherwise, this dream and this promise were never fully realized. Instead of Palestine's being given to Israel and set aside as a home for the nation, the Arabs, the direct descendants of Ishmael, were permitted to remain in the land together with the seed of Isaac. Thus we have the history of the tent of Abraham repeated.

If only the nations had kept their promise to set aside the Holy Land as a national refuge and return it to its rightful possessors, God might have raised many more of the seed of Jacob like Dr. Weizmann to bring additional blessing and help to the nations of the world. I am positive in my own mind that had the nations kept their promise, World War II would never have broken out.

All of this, of course, is repetition of the history of the tent of Abraham. Abraham had, among other children, Ishmael, the first-born, and Isaac, who was the son of promise. As long as Ishmael was alone in the tent of Abraham, there was no difficulty. But as soon as Isaac the son of promise, was born to Abraham, God's Word was, "Cast out this bondwoman and her son . . . for in Isaac shall thy seed be called." At first Abraham refused, but God made it very clear to him that Isaac and Ishmael could not live together in the same tent.

Isaac was the father of Israel, and Ishmael was the father of the Ishmaelites. The present-day Arabs are the direct descendants of Ishmael, the first-born of Abraham. They were in the land first because Ishmael was born before Isaac; but God had promised the land to Isaac, the son of the Covenant. Historically that experience is being repeated. The land has been promised as a homeland for the descendants of Isaac through Jacob, but there has been trouble ever since, because Ishmael has occupied the land, not only before Isaac's coming but also after Isaac's re-establishment in the land. The Palestinian problem will continue until, in obedience to God, the sons of the bondwoman are put out to make way for the sons of promise.

The Division of the Land

After the default of the Balfour Declaration and the failure to set aside all of Palestine as the exclusive national home for Israel, probably the greatest mistake of all history was made. In taking up this tragic error may I state that we are not trying to be critical in any way or to find fault; we are merely seeking to set forth the teaching of the Word in the hope that it may come to the attention of some who are in a position to do something about it, in order that God's plan, which can never be ignored, might be carried out.

Because of the continual fighting of the Jews and the Arabs, the land of Palestine has been divided in an effort to quiet the unrest. The Word of God is definitely clear in stating that to divide the land of Palestine is to commit a crime which God will not permit to go unjudged. Let us examine the Word of the Lord concerning this division.

At the beginning of this chapter we referred to Joel, chapter 3, and we repeat the passage:

> For, behold, in those days, and in that time, when I shall bring again the captivity of Judah and Jerusalem, I will also gather all nations, and will bring them down into the valley of Jehoshaphat, and will plead with them there for my people and for my heritage Israel, whom they have scattered among the nations, and parted my land (Joel 3:1, 2).

Note very carefully the two reasons why God Himself says that He is going to judge the nations of the world: first, He will judge them because they have scattered His people among the nations. Second, He will judge them because they have parted, or divided, His land. Remember that God says, "It is my land," and this refers to the land of Palestine. The first sin, then, which many of the nations have committed, was that of persecuting and scattering God's people, and we have seen these nations go down one after another. The second great error is the partitioning of the Promised Land. Turn to Daniel 11, which describes the last act of the Antichrist, the man of sin, who will reign in the world after the Rapture of the Church.

> Thus shall he [the Antichrist] do in the most strong holds with a strange god, whom he shall acknowledge and increase with glory: and he shall cause them to rule over many, and shall divide the land for gain (Dan. 11:39).

Then follows immediately the record of God's judgment upon this Man of Sin and of his ultimate ruin, all because of the particular sin of dividing the land. May I repeat, the judgment of God is pronounced upon the Man of Sin immediately following the statement that he "shall divide the land for gain."

According to the clear teaching of the Word of God, the next event in His program will be the catching away of the Church of the Lord Jesus. Then the Man of Sin, the Antichrist, symbolized by Nimrod, Nebuchadnezzar, and the Caesars, will appear on the scene. He will, first of all, promise to restore the nation of Israel to their land. When he has by deception gained their confidence, he will turn upon them in the midst of that Tribulation period and will, according to Scripture, repeat the sin of dividing the land of Palestine.

When the Antichrist stretches out his hand to touch that which is holy, that which God has called "my land," it will be the occasion for the coming of God's judgment upon the Man of Sin, upon his armies, and upon his entire program. He will be miserably destroyed at the coming of the Lord Jesus Christ in power and great glory. It is well to remember this, because it is taught in type as well as in direct statement throughout the Scriptures. Remember that Belshazzar, who was a type of this coming Man of Sin, made the great mistake of stretching forth his hand to touch the thing which God had called holy.

Oh, that we might see the day when the nations would turn over to the true possessors of the land of Palestine their full rights and thereby receive the blessing of the Lord! Let us pray that God may give wisdom to our leaders, that we may not invite the judgment of Almighty God, which He has pronounced upon all those who touch the things which God has called holy—His people and His land.

God's Chosen People

We have gone into considerable detail in order that we might set before you what we believe to be, according to

the Word of God, the basic problem of the world today—
the hoped-for, longed-for, and sought-for peace for which
man is striving. Israel is still God's chosen nation. By this
we do not mean that they, as individuals, can be saved
without the Lord Jesus Christ. They, too, must come as individual sinners and receive His finished work. We mean
that as a nation, in God's national dealings, they are still
His chosen people.

Palestine, the Holy Land, is also still God's chosen land;
and there can be no peace in this world until the nation
and the land, according to God's purpose, are again fully
united. Every effort for peace, the wisdom and sincerity of
the diplomats, and the endless bloodshed will never bring
about a government which will assure lasting tranquillity
and prosperity. Only as the nation of the covenant is back
in the covenant land and as the Messiah is their King will
the time come when they will beat their swords into
plowshares and their spears into pruning hooks.

The key to lasting peace is the land of Israel and the
Israel of the land. The Lord has commanded us to "pray
for the peace of Jerusalem: they shall prosper that love
thee." When Jerusalem is at peace, the world will be at
peace. Let us pray, therefore, that the leaders of the nations and our own nation may see that God is on the side
of those who recognize this program. We believe that the
wars that have been ravaging the world and causing the
utter destruction of many of the nations which have
vowed to exterminate Israel and are seeking to conquer
Palestine will ultimately come to an end. Soon the day
will come when Christ will have dominion over land and
sea.

We have tried to set before you God's program. Not in
vain has He said, "Pray for the peace of Jerusalem: they
shall prosper that love thee." The word *Jerusalem* means
"the city of peace." Basically the meaning is "the foun-

dation for peace." Notice that the meaning of the word *Jersualem* is "the foundation for peace." As long as Jerusalem is not at peace, the world cannot be at peace. Only as Jerusalem is at peace will peace prevail upon the earth. Let us pray that the time may soon come. Let us pray for our leaders. Let us pray for our nation and for the nations of the world, that they may recognize God's program and that the day may soon be ushered in when every man will sit under his own vine and his own fig tree, and the nations will "learn war" no more.

Very soon, we believe, from all indications about us, He who said He would come will come. Then we shall see the fulfillment and the vindication of the promises of God, which man has forgotten, but which will, nevertheless, be fulfilled in every detail.

(Reprinted from *The Jew and Palestine in Prophecy*, by M. R. DeHaan, by permission from the Zondervan Publishing House, Grand Rapids, Michigan)

THE GREAT PROPHECY OF THE SEVENTY WEEKS

H. A. Ironside

THE MOST REMARKABLE time prophecy of the Holy Scriptures is found in chapter 9 of the Book of Daniel. Sir Edward Denny was perhaps the first prophetic student to designate this chapter "the backbone of prophecy." Although he may have borrowed the term from someone else, I have never found it used by anyone who wrote earlier than he did. The term is well given, for if we understand the outline indicated here, we shall find that all the prophetic Scriptures fall into place so simply and harmoniously as to make it evident that we have here the backbone of the entire prophetic system of the Bible.

Those who have given much study to the Book of Daniel will remember that the chapter begins with an account of Daniel's personal exercises. He tells us that he had been studying the books of some of the prophets who had gone before him. He refers to the Book of Jeremiah for one (29:10-14) and probably the Second Book of Chronicles (36:21) for another. In these books he learned that God would accomplish seventy years in the desolations of Jerusalem. It had been definitely foretold that following the destruction of the city and the Temple and the enslavement of God's earthly people in Babylon, a period of seventy years would elapse before they would be restored to their own land and would be permitted to rebuild the Temple and eventually the city of Jerusalem itself.

Daniel had been carried away in his youth in one of the first campaigns against Palestine. As an old man he realized that the seventy-year cycle must be nearly completed, and it stirred his heart to prayer. This in itself is most suggestive. How often people take up the study of prophecy from a purely intellectual standpoint, yet surely there is nothing that should move our hearts toward God like occupation with His marvelous purpose in regard to the coming of His own blessed Son into the world again and the setting up of His glorious kingdom.

Daniel felt in his soul that the people were not in a fit state for restoration, and he took the place of confession before God. He himself was perhaps one of the holiest men living at that time; yet as he prostrated himself before the Lord, he identified himself with the sins of his people, crying, "We have sinned." As he poured out his heart in contrition, he counted on God to bring about deliverance. In answer to Daniel's prayer a messenger was sent from the throne of God, even Gabriel himself, the same glorious being who appeared to him on a later occasion and who at the beginning of New Testament times was chosen to convey to the blessed Virgin Mary the wondrous news that she was to be the destined mother of the promised Messiah.

The way in which the Spirit of God directs attention to the time when Gabriel first appeared to Daniel is interesting. We are told that he touched him "about the time of the evening oblation." That was the time when, if things had been right in Israel, the evening sacrifice would have been offered on the altar at Jerusalem; but that altar was cast down, and the Temple was in ruins. No smoke of sacrifice ascended to God from that holy place. Yet Daniel never forgot the time when the oblation should have been placed upon the altar.

That offering spoke of the sacrifice of our Lord Jesus,

which was yet to take place. God Himself saw in every victim placed on Jewish altars a type of the person and work of His own beloved Son. Everything that God will yet accomplish for Israel, for the Church, and for the nations will be based upon the finished work of Calvary's cross. Our Lord there "tasted death for every man." The last word is actually in the neuter gender in the original. Our Lord tasted death for every "thing." The blessing of the entire universe is contingent upon the work which He accomplished on the cross.

Gabriel's Message

Now let us note the message, or the prophecy, that Gabriel brought to Daniel.

> Seventy weeks are determined upon thy people and upon thy holy city, to finish the transgression, and to make an end of sins, and to make reconciliation for iniquity, and to bring in everlasting righteousness, and to seal up the vision and prophecy, and to anoint the most Holy. Know therefore and understand, that from the going forth of the commandment to restore and to build Jerusalem unto the Messiah the Prince shall be seven weeks, and threescore and two weeks: the street shall be built again, and the wall, even in troublous times.
>
> And after threescore and two weeks shall Messiah be cut off, but not for himself: and the people of the prince that shall come shall destroy the city and the sanctuary; and the end thereof shall be with a flood, and unto the end of the war desolations are determined. And he shall confirm the convenant with many for one week: and in the midst of the week he shall cause the sacrifice and the oblation to cease, and for the overspreading of abominations he shall make it desolate, even until the consummation, and that determined shall be poured upon the desolate (Dan. 9:24-27).

There are a few statements here which become a little

clearer if we turn to other translations. For instance, the Revised Version of verse 25 reads: "It shall be built again, with street and moat, even in troublous times." In place of *troublous times* some versions use the words *the narrow times*. In verse 26 the marginal reading seems better than the Revised text: "After the sixty-two weeks shall Messiah be cut off, and shall have nothing." The latter part of verse 26 is given in the Revised Version as follows: "Even unto the end shall be war; desolations are determined." In verse 27 the last half of the verse reads in the Revised Version: "Upon the wing of abominations shall one come that maketh desolate." Other slight differences are found in various versions, but they need not concern us now.

Let us weigh carefully just what is revealed here. In the first place, remember that Daniel had understood by books the number of the years in which God would accomplish the desolations of Jerusalem. His prayer of confession was given with that in view. God meets him by informing him through His angel that not at the expiration of seventy years but at the close of seventy weeks will all of Israel's sorrows come to an end. The word translated "week" is recognized by scholars generally as a generic term simply meaning "a seven." It could be used for seven days, seven months, or as is undoubtedly the case here, seven years, since it was of years that Daniel was thinking. Seventy weeks of years, then, would be 490 years.

Now let us observe exactly what the angel says. "Seventy sevens are determined," or "cut off" (cut off from the entire period of time). These seventy sevens, or 490 years, are set apart in the divine reckoning for what the angel calls "the people and thy holy city"—that is, Daniel's people, the Jews, and his holy city, Jerusalem, which was the literal capital of the land of Palestine.

What will take place at the expiration of this period of

490 years? The angel adds: "To finish the transgression, and to make an end of sins, and to make reconciliation [or atonement] for iniquity, and to bring in everlasting righteousness, and to seal up the vision and prophecy, and to anoint the most Holy."

Notice carefully each of these expressions. At the end of 490 years Israel's transgression will be finished, and their sins will be brought to an end, because their Messiah will have made reconciliation, or atonement, for iniquity. The long period of Israel's sufferings under the heel of the Gentiles will be completed, and everlasting righteousness will be brought in. This refers clearly to the setting up of Messiah's kingdom. Then the vision and the prophecy will be sealed. All will be fulfilled. Vision and prophecy will no longer be needed.

Finally, "the most Holy" will be anointed. This undoubtedly refers to the shekinah glory's returning to Israel when the people are regathered in their own land and Jehovah's temple is rebuilt. The glory has been missing ever since the destruction of Jerusalem by Nebuchadnezzar. It was not seen in the temple of Zerubbabel or in the temple of Herod, but it will return when Israel's mourning is ended and when, as a repentant people, they are brought back to God. Thus far, then, we have seen the promise of verse 24.

If we can find out just when the 490-year period was to begin, it ought to be an easy thing for us to count 490 years from that point and then to ask ourselves, "Have all these promises been fulfilled?" The starting point is given in the next verse. "Know therefore and understand, that from the going forth of the commandment to restore and to build Jerusalem. . . ." This is clearly the time from which we are to begin to count.

When did a commandment go forth for the restoration and rebuilding of Jerusalem? In this matter there is a difference of opinion among sober teachers of prophecy. Some insist that the reference is to the commandment given in the seventh chapter of the Book of Ezra, which was approximately 457 B.C. A careful examination of that decree will make it evident that it did not really have to do with restoring and building the city of Jerusalem at all; it was a confirmation of the earlier decree of Cyrus to rebuild the temple and reinstate the worship of God in Israel. It seems far more likely that the commandment referred to is actually that given in the second chapter of the Book of Nehemiah. There we find a commandment given about 445 B.C. for the restoration and rebuilding of Jerusalem.

We are not told whether the sevens of years are to be counted according to sun time or lunar time, and for our present purpose it is not necessary that we go into the problem. Sir Robert Anderson, in his masterly work, *The Coming Prince*, has taken it up in great detail and has presented a chronological system which seems fully satisfactory, though all are not prepared to accept it. Those who are interested may consult that work at their leisure. I shall not deal with chronology as such here. I desire only to emphasize that evidently we have in Nehemiah 2 the starting point for this time prophecy.

Let us go on with the quotation of the rest of the verse: "From the going forth of the commandment to restore and to build Jerusalem unto the Messiah the Prince shall be seven weeks, and threescore and two weeks." Here, then, there are 69 weeks—not 70. In other words, there are 483 years—not 490. For some reason the angel separates the last week of seven years from the 69 which were to be completed at the coming of Messiah the Prince. These 69 weeks are divided into two periods—seven weeks (or 49 years) and 62 weeks (or 434 years). Undoubtedly the division here is made in order that our minds might be prepared for a further division between the sixty-ninth and the seventieth weeks.

"The street shall be built again, and the wall, even in troublous times." Other translations are "in the narrow" and "the straitened times." The reference is evidently to the seven weeks as distinguished from the threescore and two weeks. The former period is called "the narrow times." During those 49 years the city of Jerusalem was rebuilt and the people were regathered. Those were troublous times, but the reference is evidently not so much to the distress of the people at that time as to the fact that the city was built during the narrow period.

The 62 weeks begin immediately after the expiration of the seven weeks. We are told in verse 26: "And after threescore and two weeks shall Messiah be cut off, but not for himself" (margin: "shall have nothing"). If Sir Robert Anderson is correct in his system of chronology, this tremendous event occurred within a literal week after the exact close of the 69 weeks of years. He points out that 69 years of 360 days each expired when our Lord was welcomed into Jerusalem by the children and others who cried, "Hosanna . . . Blessed is he that cometh in the name of the Lord." However, we are not told that Messiah would be cut off at the exact time of the expiration of the 62 weeks; but "after threescore and two weeks shall Messiah be cut off."

This part of the prophecy has been fulfilled to the letter. "He came unto his own, and his own received him not." He presented Himself to Israel as their promised King—Messiah. They said, "We will not have this man to reign over us," demanding that He be crucified. Pilate asked, "Shall I crucify your King?" They exclaimed, "We have no king but Caesar." And so the Messiah for whom the nation had waited so long was crucified. Following that, if we are to take the seventieth week as an immediate continuation of the period which ended at the cross, in seven years from the time of the Saviour's crucifixion all the promises made to Israel should have been fulfilled.

But they were not fulfilled. The Israelites did not recognize their Messiah. They do not know Him yet as their Sin-bearer. Their transgression has not been finished. An end of sins for them has not been made. They do not yet know anything of atonement for iniquity. Everlasting righteousness has not been brought in. Vision and prophecy have not been sealed. The "most Holy" has not been anointed by the return of the shekinah. Has the prophecy failed? Has God's Word been proved to be false? Impossible! We know that He cannot deny Himself. But it is here that we find one of the most important truths of the Word.

THE GREAT PARENTHESIS

Between the sixty-ninth and the seventieth weeks there is a parenthesis which has lasted for more than nineteen hundred years. The seventieth week has been postponed by God Himself, who changes the times and the seasons because of the transgression of the people. The moment the Messiah died on the cross, the prophetic clock stopped. There has not been a tick from that clock for nineteen centuries. It will not begin to move again until the entire present age has come to an end and Israel has once more been taken up by God.

Let us turn again to the prophecy and see definitely what is predicted there. After the declaration to Daniel that Messiah would be cut off and would have nothing after the conclusion of the 483-year period, we read: "And the people of the prince that shall come shall destroy the city and the sanctuary; and the end thereof shall be with a flood, and unto the end of the war desolations are determined."

Exactly what is predicted here? Messiah was cut off. So far as the kingdom, long promised and expected, was con-

cerned, He had nothing. Shortly after His crucifixion the
Roman people came and destroyed the city and the sanctuary. We are not told just when this took place. Actually,
it was forty years later. Observe that it is not mentioned
here that the prince would come and destroy the city.
There is in view a prince who is yet to play a great part in
prophecy. However, he has not yet appeared; but his people (the Romans) were used as the scourge of God to
punish Israel for their sins. They destroyed Jerusalem and
the temple of Jehovah.

Then we find the present age spoken of in these lines:
"The end thereof shall be with a flood, and unto the end
of the war desolations are determined" (margin: "unto the
end wars and desolations are determined"). As by an over-
flowing flood the people of Israel were to be destroyed by
their enemies, scattered throughout the world, and until
the end (the seventieth week), which remains unfulfilled,
there shall be wars and desolations. That is exactly what
our Saviour Himself tells us in Matthew 24. Throughout
the present age "ye shall hear of wars and rumors of wars:
see that ye be not troubled: for all these things must come
to pass, but the end is not yet." That end is the seventieth
week.

Throughout the Book of Daniel we find the expression,
the time of the end. That same expression is found elsewhere in the prophetic Scriptures. The time of the end is
the last seven years which God has allotted to the Jews,
which has not yet begun to run its course. As we continue
we shall see what God is doing in this intervening period
which we have designated "The Great Parenthesis."

When this time of waiting comes to an end, the prince
whose people have already appeared will come into view.
He is the great Roman leader of the last days, called in
Revelation 13 "the beast," because he is the embodiment
of every evil principle in all the empires of the world.

When he appears, he will pretend at first to be the friend of the Jews. "He shall confirm the covenant with many for one week: and in the midst of the week he shall cause the sacrifice and the oblation to cease, and for the overspreading of abominations he shall make it desolate, even until the consummation, and that determined shall be poured upon the desolate" (margin: "desolator").

Many have supposed that it was Messiah Himself who was to confirm a covenant for one week. But when did He ever make such a covenant? The blood of the covenant which He shed upon the cross is not to confirm a covenant for seven years, but it is the blood of the everlasting covenant.

In the last days, when God takes up Israel again and is about to bring her into the fullness of blessing, a Roman prince will arise who will make a covenant with the nation for seven years, promising them protection and liberty in religion as they return to their land. For three and one-half years he will permit this to go on, but in the midst of the week he will violate the covenant and demand that all worship of Jehovah cease. Then he (the Antichrist) will be manifested in his true character. This will result in what is known in Scripture as the "time of Jacob's trouble," or the Great Tribulation. It will go on for three and one-half years, until judgment is visited upon the desolator and God's earthly people are delivered.

The greater part of the Book of Revelation, virtually everything from chapter 4 to the end of chapter 19, has to do with events which will take place in Heaven and on earth during this unfulfilled seventieth week of Daniel. When this is understood, all is in harmony, and the prophetic Scriptures are plain.

(Reprinted from *The Great Parenthesis*, by H. A. Ironside, by permission from the Zondervan Publishing House, Grand Rapids, Michigan)

THE RAPTURE AND THE FIRST RESURRECTION

William L. Pettingill

WHAT DOES: "THE RAPTURE" mean? The Greek lexicon will show you that the word *rapture* is derived from the word which means "to be caught up." The use of the word in connection with the study of prophecy is based upon verses 13 to 18 of I Thessalonians 4.

> But I would not have you to be ignorant, brethren, concerning them which are asleep, that ye sorrow not, even as others which have no hope: for if we believe that Jesus died and rose again, even so them also which sleep in Jesus will God bring with him. For this we say unto you by the word of the Lord, that we which are alive and remain unto the coming of the Lord shall not prevent [precede] them which are asleep. For the Lord himself shall descend from heaven with a shout, with the voice of the archangel, and with the trump of God: and the dead in Christ shall rise first: then we which are alive and remain shall be caught up together with them in the clouds to meet the Lord in the air: and so shall we ever be with the Lord. Wherefore comfort one another with these words.

There is no question, I believe, as to the date of this epistle. All agree that it was Paul's very first contribution to the New Testament, and many believe that of all the books of the New Testament it was the first one written. We shall, therefore, make no mistake in beginning here. It is evident that I Thessalonians was written in reply to hard questions sent from Thessalonica to Paul by Timothy, his friend and fellow laborer. Chapter 17 of Acts and chapter 3 of I Thessalonians will make this clear. Paul had labored in Thessalonica only two or three weeks when his enemies drove him out of the city. After his departure many perplexing problems confronted the young converts there. Paul had taught them that when they turned to God from idols, it was "to serve the living and true God; and to wait for his Son from heaven" (I Thess. 1:9, 10). He had not talked much about the death of believers, but since he had gone from them, some of their number had died. Through Timothy they sent an inquiry to Paul concerning these Christians who had died. What had become of them? What should be their relation to the ever-imminent event of which he had told them—the catching away of the Church to meet her Lord?

First Thessalonians is Paul's answer to this and other questions. The dead in Christ were with their Lord, and those who would be alive and remaining should in no wise precede them when the Lord should come for His own. That coming for His own was something for which to wait constantly. It might take place at any time. Their duty was to serve and to wait. All through the epistle these things are stressed, and in most of the later epistles of Paul to the churches they were among the subjects treated. Nothing is more insisted upon than the attitude of expectancy in view of the imminent Rapture of the church.

The Rapture of the church, as is seen from the Scripture already quoted, is linked with the resurrection of the saved. I say "of the saved," for the lost will not be raised from the dead at the same time with the saved. The resurrection of the saved "is the first resurrection," as Revelation 20:5 tells us. The whole passage reads as follows:

And I saw thrones, and they [the armies of heaven—19:14] sat upon them, and judgment was given unto them: and I saw the souls of them that were beheaded for the witness of Jesus, and for the word of God, and which had not worshipped the beast [the wicked king of chapter 13], neither his image, neither had received his mark upon their foreheads, or in their hands; and they lived [literally, lived again, or revived] and reigned with Christ a thousand years.

Here it is proper to explain that the word *millennium* means "a thousand years." It comes to us through the Latin *mille*, meaning "a thousand," and *annum*, meaning "year."

But the rest of the dead lived not again until the thousand years were finished. This is the first resurrection. Blessed and holy is he that hath part in the first resurrection: on such the second death hath no power, but they shall be priests of God and of Christ, and shall reign with him a thousand years (Rev. 20:5, 6).

Then follows a description of what comes after the Millennium.

There are, then, two resurrections instead of one, and the two are separated from each other by a thousand years. The first resurrection is premillennial, or before the Millennium. The second resurrection is postmillennial, or after the Millennium. The first resurrection is only for the saved; the second resurrection is only for the lost.

But now we need to turn to chapter 5 of John to clear up a point in connection with this part of our subject. Here in verse 24 a resurrection—that is, a coming to life from the dead—is described, but it is spiritual resurrection. "Verily, verily, I say unto you, He that heareth my word, and believeth on him that sent me, hath everlasting life, and shall not come into condemnation; but is passed from death unto life."

This is spiritual resurrection, clearly enough; it is what takes place when a man is born again. We also find this in the next verse.

> Verily, verily, I say unto you, The hour is coming, and now is, when the dead shall hear the voice of the Son of God: and they that hear shall live.

BODILY AND SPIRITUAL RESURRECTION

This is spiritual resurrection also; for the Lord said, "The hour is coming, and now is." Bodily resurrection has not taken place yet, but spiritual resurrection now is possible. Every time the Gospel is preached to lost men—and the Gospel is certainly "the voice of the Son of God"—it is preached to those who are dead in their trespasses and sins. Some will, by the power of the grace of God, hear that voice; and they that hearken will live. That is spiritual resurrection. It is coming from death unto life; yet it is not bodily resurrection.

Now let us go to John 5:28, 29. There we shall find bodily resurrection.

> Marvel not at this: for the hour is coming, in the which all that are in the graves shall hear his voice, and shall come forth; they that have done good, unto the resurrection of life; and they that have done evil, unto the resurrection of damnation.

Standing by itself this statement would seem to teach the resurrection of all, both saved and lost, at the same time. But let it be noted that the "hour" of verse 25 has already lasted for nineteen hundred years. Why, then should not the "hour" of verse 28 endure throughout the thousand years of the Millennium? Even here in verse 29 two resurrections are named—one unto life and one unto damnation. In Luke 14:14 the first resurrection is called "the resurrection of the just."

There are hints in the teaching of the Lord Jesus which seem to show how His own mind was often occupied with anticipation of that great day of the Rapture of the Church and the resurrection of His beloved ones. For example, between Christ's words in the opening verses of John 14 and Paul's words in chapter 4 of I Thessalonians there is a parallelism that can easily be traced.

Our Lord said, "Let not your heart be troubled." Paul said, "Comfort one another with these words."

The Lord said, "Ye believe in God, believe also in me." Paul said, "If we believe that Jesus died and rose again, even so them also which sleep in Jesus will God bring with him."

The Lord said, "If it were not so, I would have told you." Paul said, "This we say unto you by the word of the Lord" (literally, "by a word from the Lord"; that is, from Jesus' own mouth).

The Lord said, "I will come again." Paul said, "The Lord himself shall descend from heaven."

The Lord said, "And receive you unto myself." Paul said, "We . . . shall be caught up . . . to meet the Lord in the air."

The Lord said, "That where I am, there ye may be also." Paul said, "And so shall we ever be with the Lord."

The parallel is too complete to be accidental. It is of the Spirit of God.

There is another such parallelism in connection with I Corinthians 15:51-54, a passage so familiar as to have lost its point with many who seem to think that it has no important place outside the funeral ritual. But let us look at it as something new, just as if we had never seen it before. Let us place ourselves by imagination in the home of Aquila and Priscilla on the night when probably the church at Corinth met in their house to hear the latest news of their beloved Paul (I Cor. 16:19). The meeting came to order, and someone announced that there was a letter from the apostle to be read to the assembly. Imagine, if you can, the tremendous impact when the startling words were read: "Behold, I show you a mystery; we shall not all sleep."

In modern phraseology this means, "Listen! I have a secret to tell you. Not all of us will die!"

Whatever could the man mean? Everybody knows that we must all die. But that is the great mystery now revealed—the wonderful secret never before made known.

> Behold, I show you a mystery; we shall not all sleep, but we shall all be changed. In a moment, in the twinkling of an eye, at the last trump: for the trumpet shall sound, and the dead shall be raised incorruptible, and we shall be changed. For this corruptible must put on incorruption [literally, incorruptibility], and this mortal must put on immortality. So when this corruptible shall have put on incorruption [literally, incorruptibility], and this mortal shall have put on immortality, then shall be brought to pass the saying that is written, Death is swallowed up in victory.

For the parallelism let us turn to John 11:20-26 and note carefully the language.

> Then Martha, as soon as she heard that Jesus was coming, went and met him: but Mary sat still in the house. Then said Martha unto Jesus, Lord, if thou hadst been here, my brother had not died. But I know, that even now, whatsoever thou wilt ask of God, God will give it thee. Jesus saith unto her, Thy brother shall rise again. Martha saith unto him, I know that he shall rise again in the resurrection at the last day. Jesus said unto her, I am the resurrection, and the life: he that believeth in me, though he were dead [literally, though he die], yet shall he live: and whosoever liveth and believeth in me shall never die. Believest thou this?

Here is language that confuses the commentators and defies all intelligent or intelligible exposition until the parallelism is seen to which reference has been made. It is as clear as the noonday sun that the Lord Jesus, who was about to enact a miniature representation of "the resurrection at the last day," had the scenes of that day in mind while He was talking to Martha.

When the day arrives—the day of the first resurrection—He who is the resurrection and the life will do on a large scale what He did in the Bethany burying ground when He called His friend Lazarus out of the grave. But He will also do much more than raise dead men to life. On the great day that is coming He will speak out of Heaven the word of power, and "he that believeth in" Him, "though he were dead, yet shall he live." As Paul puts it, "The dead shall be raised incorruptible."

As for those other believers, those who "are alive and remain," our Lord declares, "Whosoever liveth and believeth in me shall never die." Again the parallel is complete. It is impossible to regard it as accidental. It fits as a hand in a glove. It is of God's Spirit.

Death does not await all of God's children. Some will not die. The Lord Jesus may at any moment say, "Come up hither" (Rev. 4:1), and He will draw His own—the living and the dead—up to Himself in the air. For this we are to look, for this we are to wait, and in this hope we are to live. Blessed hope! How it should lay hold upon us! How it should mold our lives! What a pity that we have not learned it and have not been gripped by it! It is written that "every man that hath this hope in him purifieth himself, even as he is pure." May it be so with each one who reads this chapter. May every day be lived in the power of the God-given truth that before the day is ended we may be "caught up . . . to meet the Lord in the air!"

Caught up! Caught up! No wing required!
Caught up to Him, by love inspired,
    To meet Him in the air!
Spurning the earth with upward bound,
Nor casting a single glance around,
Nor listing a single earth-born sound,
    Caught up in the radiant air!
Caught up with rapture and surprise!
Caught up! Our fond affections rise
    Our coming Lord to meet!
Hearing the trumpet's glorious sound,
Soaring to join the rising crowd,
Gazing beyond the parted cloud,
    Beneath His piercéd feet!

(Reprinted from *God's Prophecies for Plain People*, by
William L. Pettingill, by permission of Van Kampen Press,
Wheaton, Illinois)

THE TRIBULATION

H. A. Ironside

THOSE WHO ATTACK dispensational truth tell us that the Great Tribulation is in the past. They declare that the truth which we have been teaching people for years—that the dispensation of grace, now on the verge of closing, will be followed by the Great Tribulation—is all wrong. They say that it is just a fantastic notion that is unsupported by Scripture. Is the Tribulation in the past, or is it in the future? Let us turn to God's Word for the answer to this question.

First we must speak briefly of the seventy weeks of Daniel 9. Having been familiar with these things for thirty-three years and having examined very carefully much that has been written contrary thereto, I am absolutely convinced that the seventieth week of Daniel is yet unfulfilled. It is the only view that, to my mind, harmonizes with all the prophecies in Scripture. It makes the Book of Revelation perfectly clear. It explains the difficult things in the Book of Daniel and other prophetic books.

Until one sees the break between the sixty-ninth and the seventieth week, all is confusion. The Great Tribulation is to occur in this seventieth week. I want to show that this is clearly taught in the Word.

Those who teach that the Tribulation was in the past are divided into several distinct schools. The Preterists maintain that the Great Tribulation took place at the time of the trouble which the Jewish people passed through when the Roman armies, under Titus, destroyed Jerusa-

lem and wrought havoc throughout Palestine. The Great
Tribulation, according to them, began in A.D. 70 and ended
a very short time afterward. The Roman Catholic view
which is ordinarily held refers to the two hundred or more
years of persecution under pagan Rome, which ended
with the church's triumph over the paganism of the
empire.

The other view, commonly known as the historical interpretation, holds that the Great Tribulation referred to
the period of trial during which those who protested
against the Romish dogmas were persecuted.

Those who are called Futurists maintain that the
Great Tribulation has never yet taken place and cannot
begin as long as the Church of God (born-again believers) is in the world. It will not take place until we have
been called to meet the Lord in the air. This is the view
that I hold.

We shall now turn to some passages of Scripture and
see whether or not it is logically possible to believe that
the Great Tribulation is in the past.

In the opening verses of Jeremiah 30 we have a prophecy in regard to the restoration of Israel to the land of
Palestine. Scripture shows that they are restored, still in
unbelief, to the land of Palestine. Conviction and re-
generation take place after the restoration to the land of
Palestine, when the Church has been caught up.

In Jeremiah 30:3 we read:

> For, lo, the days come, saith the Lord, that I will
> bring again the captivity of my people Israel and Judah,
> saith the Lord: and I will cause them to return to the
> land that I gave to their fathers, and they shall pos-
> sess it.

This does not refer to the temporary return under Ezra
and Nehemiah. "They shall possess it" indicates that they

will enter into possession of the land, not to surrender it
again to any other people.

In verses 4-7 we have a description of the hour of trial
that is coming upon the land.

> And these are the words that the Lord spake concern-
> ing Israel and concerning Judah. For thus saith the Lord;
> We have heard a voice of trembling, of fear, and not of
> peace. Ask ye now, and see whether a man doth travail
> with child? wherefore do I see every man with his hands
> on his loins, as a woman in travail, and all faces are
> turned into paleness? Alas! for that day is great, so that
> none is like it: it is even the time of Jacob's trouble, but
> he shall be saved out of it.

Observe that this is not the time of the Church's trouble;
it has nothing whatsoever to do with the Church. It is the
time of Jacob's trouble. What must be the result? That
Jacob is scattered and broken and practically destroyed?
No, the very opposite! He is saved out of it. The Great
Tribulation will end with the deliverance rather than the
scattering of Israel. That does not fit in at all with what
took place in the land of Palestine in A.D. 70 and the years
that followed. Instead of being saved out of it, Jacob was
scattered throughout the entire world as a result of it.

> For it shall come to pass in that day, saith the Lord
> of hosts, that I will break his yoke [the yoke of the
> Gentiles] from off thy neck, and will burst thy bonds,
> and strangers shall no more serve themselves of him
> (Jer. 30:8).

They will no more make a servant of him, for he is the
true son of David.

> Therefore fear thou not, O my servant Jacob, saith
> the Lord; neither be dismayed, O Israel: for, lo, I will
> save thee from afar, and thy seed from the land of their
> captivity; and Jacob shall return, and shall be in rest,

and be quiet, and none shall make him afraid (Jer. 30:10).

Daniel 11 gives us a very remarkable prophecy that reaches right down to the end of the Jewish dispensation, to the "time of the end," which is a term used again and again. We read of Israel's sorrows and sufferings under the Antichrist. There is a description of the Antichrist in Daniel 11:36-39:

> The king shall do according to his will; and he shall exalt himself, and magnify himself above every god, and shall speak marvelous things against the God of gods, and shall prosper till the indignation be accomplished.

We read in Daniel 12:1:

> And at that time shall Michael stand up, the great prince which standeth for the children of thy people: and there shall be a time of trouble, such as never was since there was a nation even to that same time: and at that time thy people shall be delivered, every one that shall be found written in the book.

Is it not true that there has never been a time of more dreadful suffering than that which Israel endured under Rome? Read what Josephus says about the horror which the people of Israel endured in those days. Many think that this might be the time referred to. But notice the last part of the verse:

> And at that time thy people shall be delivered, every one that shall be found written in the book.

They were not delivered at the time of the Roman persecution; instead, they were scattered everywhere throughout the world. It is clear that this continues until the kingdom.

> And many of them that sleep in the dust of the earth

shall awake, some to everlasting life, and some to shame
and everlasting contempt (Dan. 12:2).

Some do not think that this is the literal resurrection. It
may be the picture we have in the Book of Ezekiel of the
dry bones of Israel springing into life, coming up from
the dust of the earth (from being scattered among the
Gentiles), some to everlasting life, and those who are
apostate, to shame and everlasting contempt.

They that be wise shall shine as the brightness of the
firmament; and they that turn many to righteousness as
the stars for ever and ever (Dan. 12:3).

To what time does this refer?

But thou, O Daniel, shut up the words, and seal the
book, even to the time of the end: many shall run to and
fro, and knowledge shall be increased (Dan. 12:4).

One sign of the time of the end is that people will run
to and fro throughout the world, and there will be an increase of knowledge.

Commenting on these words more than one hundred
years ago, Sir Isaac Newton said, "Personally, I cannot
but believe these words concerning the end of the times.
One sign of the end will be a remarkable increase in
methods of getting about. Men will travel from country
to country in an unprecedented manner. There may be
some inventions which will enable people to travel much
more quickly than they do now." Sir Isaac Newton believed it possible that, as the end drew near, somebody
might invent a means of locomotion which would enable
people to travel at the astonishing rate of fifteen or twenty
miles an hour.

Voltaire said, "See what a fool Christianity makes of an
otherwise brilliant man! Here a scientist like Newton actually writes that men may travel at the rate of fifteen or

twenty miles an hour. Has he forgotten that if a man would travel at the rate of fifteen miles an hour, he would be suffocated? His heart would stand still." It was not long until man traveled at the speed considered fatal by Voltaire. He survived. Now men travel at astonishing speeds.

The last part of Zechariah, from chapter twelve to the end, seems to deal almost entirely with this period of great trouble. In chapter 14 we read that Jerusalem itself will be affected.

> Behold, the day of the Lord cometh, and thy spoil shall be divided in the midst of thee. For I will gather all nations against Jerusalem to battle; and the city shall be taken, and the houses rifled, and the women ravished; and half of the city shall go forth into captivity, and the residue of the people shall not be cut off from the city.

The Preterist interprets this by a system of accommodation, saying, "Were not the Roman armies the representatives of all nations, all fighting under the banner of Caesar?" That is not what we have here. Here we have the definite armies of all the nations of the world gathered together against Jerusalem in that last great effort. When this takes place, "then shall the Lord go forth, and fight against those nations, as when he fought in the day of battle."

Notice the order here—Jerusalem surrounded by the armies of the nations, a time of great distress and trouble, the people crying to God for help, and the Lord going forth to destroy the armies (we also see Him in battle in chapter 19 of Revelation) and coming down to earth. "His feet shall stand in that day upon the mount of Olives" (Jer. 14:4). The Preterist tells us that this has already been fulfilled—that His feet stood on the Mount of Olives be-

fore He went up into Heaven. But here He descends at the
close of this period of trouble, and His feet stand on the
Mount of Olives. What happens? "And the mount of
Olives shall cleave in the midst thereof toward the east
and toward the west, and there shall be a very great
valley; and half of the mountain shall remove toward the
north, and half of it toward the south."

Some years ago there was a great earthquake in Palestine. The Mount of Olives was badly shaken, and many
buildings were leveled. Some English scientists investi-
gated this. After making an examination of the geological
strata in Palestine, they said, "We have found the occasion
of the earthquake. There is a geological fault running
through the mountains of Lebanon. It is particularly evident in the Mount of Olives. There is a great shifting of
strata; and some of these days there will undoubtedly be a
greater earthquake in Palestine, as a result of which the
Mount of Olives will be torn in two." We not only knew
about that long ago, but we also know just what will make
it break in two. The blessed feet of our Saviour will again
touch this earth, and the moment He takes His stand on
the Mount of Olives there will be a great earthquake. The
Mount of Olives will be torn asunder at the close of the
Great Tribulation. Then Israel will be delivered.

Let us now turn to the New Testament (Matt. 24:21),
where we read of events that will take place before His
second coming:

> For then shall be great tribulation, such as was not
> since the beginning of the world to this time, no, nor
> ever shall be.

How manifestly He chose to use almost the identical
language that the angel used in speaking to Daniel in order that we may understand that it refers to exactly the
same event!

And except those days should be shortened, there should no flesh be saved: but for the elect's sake those days shall be shortened. Then if any man shall say unto you, Lo, here is Christ, or there; believe it not. For there shall arise false Christs, and false prophets, and shall show great signs and wonders; insomuch that, if it were possible, they shall deceive the very elect (Matt. 24: 22-24).

Men look for the return of the Lord, and all sorts of false theories are proclaimed.

For as the lightning cometh out of the east, and shineth even unto the west; so shall also the coming of the Son of man be. For wheresoever the carcase is, there will the eagles be gathered together (Matt. 24:27, 28).

The "carcase" will be Jerusalem, the apostate part of Israel found in the land of Palestine. There the vultures, the armies of all nations, will come; and while things are in this condition, the Son of Man will appear.

Immediately after the tribulation of those days shall the sun be darkened, and the moon shall not give her light, and the stars shall fall from heaven, and the powers of the heavens shall be shaken: and then shall appear the sign of the Son of man in heaven: and then shall all the tribes of the earth mourn, and they shall see the Son of man coming in the clouds of heaven with power and great glory. And he shall send his angels with a great sound of a trumpet, and they shall gather together his elect [the elect of Israel] from the four winds, from one end of heaven to the other (Matt. 24:29-31).

The Preterists interpret our Lord as depicting the desolation of Palestine under Rome, but did the events here predicted follow the desolation? The historical interpreters tell us that these events took place during the persecution of the Christians under the papacy for something like twelve and a half centuries. When the persecution came to an end after the terrible Spanish Inquisition, did these events take place? Any student of history knows the answer, which is an emphatic negative.

But let us suppose that everything in verse 29 could be spiritualized—the darkening of the sun and moon, an eclipse, the falling of the stars, a shower of meteorites, and the shaking of the powers of Heaven; or suppose that the entire verse could refer to the subduing of a great imperial power. What about verse 30? This verse tells us that the return of the Son of Man will be visible. "Then shall appear the sign of the Son of man in heaven . . . and they shall see the Son of man . . . ." While it is still possible to spiritualize this event, making the return of Christ some great spiritual experience, like a revival, we believe that this verse is much more difficult to be twisted and adapted by those who do not want to accept the plain, literal meaning. The simplest possible interpretation is to accept it just as it is.

Now turn to Luke's account and notice a very important distinction there between the Great Tribulation and the sorrows of Palestine under the Romans.

> And when ye shall see Jerusalem compassed with armies, then know that the desolation thereof is nigh (Luke 21:20).

Here, unquestionably, our Lord predicted the destruction of Jerusalem under Titus. This prophecy has been fulfilled with the strictest literality.

We can judge the future only by the past. If prophecy has had only a spiritual fulfillment in the past, it will have only a spiritual fulfillment in the future. But if prophecy has had a strictly literal fulfillment in the past, it is absolutely certain that it will have a strictly literal fulfillment in the future.

Here our Lord prophesied what will come to Jerusalem.

If you are familar with the history of the fall of Jerusalem,
you will know how definitely the events predicted came
to pass. We read, "Jerusalem compassed with armies," and
in accordance with this, three Roman armies besieged
Jerusalem.

> Then know that the desolation thereof is nigh. Then
> let them which are in Judea flee to the mountains; and
> let them which are in the midst of it depart out; and let
> not them that are in the countries enter thereinto (Luke
> 21:20, 21).

You remember that when Titus was to make his final on-
slaught, he first proclaimed an armistice and allowed anyone who desired to do so to leave the city. He appointed
Pella, a mountain city, as a place of refuge for them. Everyone who believed in the Lord Jesus Christ and honored
His name left the city. There was not a Christian left in
that siege. Our Lord gave them instructions: "When ye
shall see [this] . . . flee," and they went to Pella for
protection.

> For these be the days of vengeance, that all things
> which are written may be fulfilled. But woe unto them
> that are with child, and to them that give suck, in those
> days! for there shall be great distress in the land, and
> wrath upon this people. And they shall fall by the edge
> of the sword, and shall be led away captive into all na-
> tions: and Jerusalem shall be trodden down of the Gen-
> tiles, until the times of the Gentiles be fulfilled.

Did this tribulation under Titus result in the deliverance of Israel? No, it resulted in the scattering of Israel.
Israel was led captive of all nations. Very well, what about
the centuries since?

> Jerusalem shall be trodden down of the Gentiles, until
> the times of the Gentiles be fulfilled.

Here is a long period during which Jerusalem, the land of Palestine, and the people of Israel are under Gentile dominion. That period is known as "the times of the Gentiles," and it will run until its fulfillment. Then what? How will they know when they have come to the end of that period?

And there shall be signs in the sun, and in the moon, and in the stars; and upon the earth distress of nations, with perplexity; the sea and the waves roaring . . . And then shall they see the Son of man coming in a cloud with power and great glory (Luke 21:25, 27).

So the Tribulation will come at the end of the times of the Gentiles and will close with the descent of the Lord from Heaven.

What will charaterize the time of the Tribulation? It will be the day of Antichrist. The Thessalonians were perplexed and troubled because of the sufferings through which they were passing, and they feared that already they were in the time of the Great Tribulation, which is called "the Day of the Lord's Vengeance." Paul wrote in II Thessalonians 2:

Now we beseech you, brethren, by the coming of our Lord Jesus Christ, and by our gathering together unto him, that ye be not soon shaken in mind, or be troubled, neither by spirit, nor by word, nor by letter as from us [someone had evidently forged a letter from Paul telling them that the Tribulation was already upon them] as that the day of Christ is at hand. Let no man deceive you by any means: for that day shall not come, except there come a falling away first, and that man of sin be revealed, the son of perdition; who opposeth and exalteth himself above all that is called God, or that is worshiped; so that he as God sitteth in the temple of God, showing himself that he is God.

Someone might say, "The Great Tribulation began

when Gregory declared himself to be the head of all the churches of Christendom; therefore, it refers to the papal persecution." However, we have seen that the Great Tribulation will end with the deliverance of Israel and the visible return of our Lord to this earth, a return so literal that His feet will stand in that day on the Mount of Olives. Surely this cannot refer to the papacy, "who opposeth and exalteth himself above all that is called God, or that is worshiped; so that he as God sitteth in the temple of God, showing himself that he is God." If this referred to the papacy, the pope would have to sit in the temple of God. I do not believe that St. Peter's Cathedral is the temple of God. It is a temple of idolatry. Nor do I believe that the Roman church is the temple of God. It is an apostate system. But the temple of God is the temple frequently spoken of by the prophets as the temple yet to be built. The Antichrist sits there and declares himself to be God.

> Remember ye not, that, when I was yet with you, I told you these things? And now ye know what withholdeth that he might be revealed in his time. For the mystery of iniquity doth already work: only he who now letteth will let, until he be taken out of the way (II Thess. 2:5-7).

Some think this meant that the Roman Empire would be dissolved first. Paul was talking about something here that every Christian ought to know, because the Bible reveals it. What hinders full development of evil in the world? The Spirit of God restrains now. The Spirit of God is here in the Church of God, restraining the full development of evil. Some day the Church will be gone, and the Spirit of God will no longer be active on earth as a divine Person in the Church of God.

> And then shall that Wicked be revealed, whom the Lord shall consume with the spirit of his mouth, and

shall destroy with the brightness of his coming: even him, whose coming is after the working of Satan with all power and signs and lying wonders (II Thess. 2:8, 9).

These signs and lying wonders are pictured in Revelation 13.

What will be the outcome when the Tribulation comes upon the earth? A large part of Revelation evidently has to do with the Great Tribulation, ending with the personal appearing of our Lord Jesus Christ. It fits so perfectly with what we read of the Great Tribulation that I am sure it is the same time. Not all of Israel are really Israel. It must be regenerated Israel in that day to be really Israel and to be so counted, just as today the Israel of God are those who are regenerated. In the first part of Revelation 7 you have the remnant of Israel.

And after these things I saw four angels standing on the four corners of the earth, holding the four winds of the earth, that the wind should not blow on the earth, nor on the sea, nor on any tree. And I saw another angel ascending from the east, having the seal of the living God: and he cried with a loud voice to the four angels, to whom it was given to hurt the earth and the sea, saying, Hurt not the earth, neither the sea, nor the trees, till we have sealed the servants of our God in their foreheads [the four angels who are seen sealing the servants of our God before the Great Tribulation begins]. And I heard the number of them which were sealed: and there were sealed an hundred and forty and four thousand of all the tribes of the children of Israel.

In the fourteenth chapter of Revelation the Saviour actually appears, and we find that the 144,000, delivered out of the Tribulation, are waiting to receive Him. They form what we might call a royal bodyguard in the coming day when He will establish His glorious millennial kingdom. Israel is sealed by God at the beginning of the

Tribulation (chap. 7). Israel is preserved for the kingdom at the end of the Tribulation (chap. 14).

The 144,000 are out of every tribe of Israel. No one can possibly be misled about this. Look at the latter part of chapter 7. I do not know whether or not the number *144,000* can be taken literally.

> After this I beheld, and, lo, a great multitude, which no man could number, of all nations, and kindreds, and people, and tongues, stood before the throne, and before the Lamb, clothed with white robes, and palms in their hands (v. 9).
>
> And one of the elders answered, saying unto me, What are these which are arrayed in white robes? and whence came they? And I [John] said unto him, Sir, thou knowest. And he said to me, These are they which came out of great tribulation, and have washed their robes, and made them white in the blood of the Lamb (vv. 13, 14).

"And have washed their robes, and made them white in the blood of the Lamb." How are people to be saved in the Tribulation day? Just exactly as they are saved today—through the same precious blood of Christ. Every soul saved in any dispensation, from the day of Abel down to the end of the Millennium, owes all of his blessing to the precious, atoning blood of the Son of God.

> Therefore are they before the throne of God, and serve him day and night in his temple: and he that sitteth on the throne shall dwell among them. They shall hunger no more, neither thirst any more; neither shall the sun light on them, nor any heat. For the Lamb which is in the midst of the throne shall feed them, and shall lead them unto living fountains of waters: and God shall wipe away all tears from their eyes (vv. 15-17).

The company saved in the Tribulation will remain on earth to share in the millennial kingdom. In Isaiah 49:8-12 we have a prophecy that refers to this very same company:

> Thus saith the Lord, In an acceptable time have I heard thee, and in a day of salvation have I helped thee: and I will preserve thee, and give thee for a covenant of the people, to establish the earth, to cause to inherit the desolate heritages; that thou mayest say to the prisoners, Go forth; to them that are in darkness, Show yourselves. They shall feed in the ways, and their pastures shall be in all high places. They shall not hunger nor thirst; neither shall the heat nor sun smite them: for he that hath mercy on them shall lead them, even by the springs of water shall he guide them. And I will make all my mountains a way, and my highways shall be exalted. Behold, these shall come from far: and, lo, these from the north and from the west; and these from the land of Sinim [the ancient name for China].

There will be a vast throng of Gentiles to whom the light will come in those dark days of the Tribulation to prepare them for the glorious kingdom of the Lord Jesus Christ.

So I think that the Scriptures looked at, and there are many more than could have been added, are sufficient surely to show us that the Great Tribulation did not take place when Jerusalem was destroyed by the Romans, nor did it take place under either pagan or papal Rome. It will occur immediately before the appearing of the Lord Jesus Christ to establish His glorious kingdom in this world. It will not take place before the Church has gone to Heaven. Five proofs of this are listed below:

1. The Tribulation cannot take place before the Lamb opens the book with seven seals. When the seals are broken, troubles begin to come (Rev. 5).

2. The Lamb does not receive the seven-sealed book from the hand of the Father until the crowned saints are seen in Heaven. In Revelation 4 and 5 we have the

twenty-four elders seated about the throne wearing crowns of gold upon their heads.

3. No saints will be crowned in Heaven until the apostle Paul receives his crown. "Henceforth there is laid up for me a crown of righteousness, which the Lord, the righteous judge, shall give me at that day: and not to me only, but unto all them also that love his appearing" (II Tim. 4:8).

4. The apostle Paul and other saints with him will not receive their crowns until the Judgment Seat of Christ. It is referred to as "that day."

5. The Judgment Seat of Christ is immediately after the Rapture of the Church. Jesus says, "Behold, I come quickly; and my reward is with me, to give every man according as his work shall be."

The conclusion, therefore, is that there will be no Great Tribulation before the Church has gone to be with the Lord. The Rapture must take place before the time of the Great Tribulation can begin here on the earth.

(Reprinted from *The Lamp of Prophecy*, by H. A. Ironside, by permission of Zondervan Publishing House, Grand Rapids, Michigan)

DANIEL'S SEVENTIETH WEEK

Theodore H. Epp

IN THIS TIME OF INSECURITY people are spending much of their time trying to solve world problems, but they are having no success. Their difficulty is that they have left God out of their plans and have tried to make their own utopia.

God will not always be patient with their neglect and rejection of Him. He has told us of a time of judgment when man's troubles will be multiplied and when he will suffer previously unknown torture and tribulation. This period of time is called the Tribulation, although it is also known as "The Great Tribulation," "The Time of Jacob's Trouble," "The Passing Under the Rod," "The Melting Pot," "The Time of Trouble for His People," and "The Great and Terrible Day of the Lord."

We believe that this time cannot be very far away, for prophecies which point toward the soon arrival of this Tribulation period are being fulfilled.

However, those who have trusted Christ as their Saviour do not have to look forward to that time, for the Tribulation period will be preceded by the Rapture of the Church. At that time all Christians, those who have had their sins washed away by the blood of Christ, will meet Him in the air and will be taken by Him to Heaven.

When the Church has been taken away, those who are left on the earth, the unsaved, will find the world suddenly cast into a chaotic condition. No man will be able to escape this time of trouble. The Tribulation will last for a period of seven years, between the dispensation of grace, the dispensation in which you and I are living today, and the Millennium, the time when Jesus will have His kingdom upon the earth.

The purpose of this Tribulation will be primarily to purify the people of Israel so that God once more can deal with them as His people. But the Gentile nations will also pass through this judgment.

THE FACT OF THE TRIBULATION

The fact of the Tribulation is definitely verified by many prophecies in the Scriptures. Jeremiah 30:4, 7 speaks of it. In Ezekiel 20:35-38 we read:

> And I will bring you [speaking of the people of Israel] into the wilderness of the people, and there will I plead with you face to face. Like as I pleaded with your fathers in the wilderness of the land of Egypt, so will I plead with you, saith the Lord God. And I will cause you to pass under the rod, and I will bring you into the bond of the covenant: and I will purge out from among you the rebels.

There is more concerning this in Ezekiel 22:17-22:

> And the word of the Lord came unto me, saying, Son of man, the house of Israel is to me become dross: all they are brass, and tin, and iron, and lead, in the midst of the furnace; they are even the dross of silver. Therefore thus saith the Lord God; because ye are all become dross, behold, therefore I will gather you into the midst of Jerusalem. As they gather silver, and brass, and iron, and lead, and tin, into the midst of the furnace, to blow the fire upon it, to melt it; so will I gather you in mine anger and in my fury, and I will leave you there, and melt you. Yea, I will gather you, and blow upon you in the fire of my wrath, and ye shall be melted in the midst

thereof. As silver is melted in the midst of the furnace, so shall ye be melted in the midst thereof; and ye shall know that I the Lord have poured out my fury upon you.

In Malachi 3:1-3 we find an additional reference to the Tribulation. In Daniel 12:1 we read:

And at that time shall Michael stand up, the great prince which standeth for the children of thy people: and there shall be a time of trouble, such as never was since there was a nation even to that same time: and at that time thy people shall be delivered, every one that shall be found written in the book.

Zechariah 13:8, 9 tells us that many of Israel will go through this Great Tribulation.

And it shall come to pass, that in all the land, saith the Lord, two parts therein shall be cut off and die; but the third shall be left therein. And I will bring the third part through the fire, and will refine them as silver is refined, and will try them as gold is tried; they shall call on my name, and I will hear them: I will say, It is my people: and they shall say, The Lord is my God.

Only one-third of the Israelites who enter the Tribulation will actually pass through it. However, I believe that this does not include the 144,000 who will be sealed. The New Testament also speaks of the Great Tribulation. In Matthew 24:15, 21 we have this description:

When ye therefore shall see the abomination of desolation, spoken of by Daniel the prophet, stand in the holy place . . . For then shall be great tribulation, such as was not since the beginning of the world to this time, no, nor ever shall be.

These, together with many other Scriptures taken from Revelation 6-19, give us the description of this Tribulation.

TIME OF THE TRIBULATION

The Tribulation begins after the Church has been taken away, when the Antichrist begins his reign on the earth. Daniel made this statement:

> And he [the Antichrist] shall confirm the covenant with many [of Israel] for one week (Dan. 9:27).

The word *week* is used here to determine a period of time known to us as seven years.

> And in the midst of the week [these seven years] he shall cause the sacrifice and the oblation to cease, and for the overspreading of abominations he shall make it desolate, even until the consummation, and that determined shall be poured upon the desolate (Dan. 9:27).

There are to be seventy weeks, or seventy periods of seven years each, for Israel. Sixty-nine of these periods were fulfilled at the time that Jesus Christ was crucified. Daniel said that when sixty-nine of these periods were fulfilled, the Messiah would be cut off, and He was. Therefore, one period of seven years still has not been fulfilled. This is the period known as the Tribulation. Concerning this time Paul said:

> For I would not, brethren, that ye should be ignorant of this mystery, lest ye should be wise in your own conceits; that blindness in part is happened to Israel, until the fullness of the Gentiles be come in (Rom. 11:25).

We have seen now that there is to be a Tribulation. It is a fact; it is described in many, many passages of Scripture. It will last seven years; it is a future time of testing and trial. It will be between the dispensation in which we are now living and the time when Christ will set up His kingdom.

PHASES OF THE TRIBULATION

Beginning with Revelation 6 there is a detailed description of what will actually take place during this Tribulation. It is divided into two periods of three and one-half years each. The last half is characterized by such great furor, chaos, and anger of God that it is known as the Great Tribulation. Such a time has never been seen upon the earth before.

During this period of seven years the seals, the trumpets, and the vials will be fulfilled. In the opening of the seals God reveals how He will permit man to see his own destruction. In trying to save himself, man destroys himself. Then the trumpets are blown; here God permits Satan to come in great wrath, bringing more destruction upon the world. In the pouring out of the vials God's wrath is revealed.

THE SEVEN SEALS

During the Tribulation period God will permit man to come to the end of himself. But man will make an attempt to bring himself out of this particular chaotic condition, and God will permit him to try. Of course, man will turn to his only course of action—war. We have seen awful wars, but during this time wars such as the world has never yet seen will be fought.

When the first seal is broken, the white horse will appear upon which the Antichrist will ride forth to conquer. Even now we see that the spirit of the Antichrist is in the communistic advances. However, the Antichrist will not be a Communist; he will be against them.

In the second seal we see the red horse, which speaks of war.

> Power was given to him that sat thereon to take peace from the earth, and that they should kill one another: and there was given unto him a great sword (Rev. 6:4).

That is followed by the third seal. Here we see that the black horse, which speaks of famine, will come immediately after this great war, or he may come during it.

Then comes the fourth seal. The pale horse speaks of death which follows famine, war, and pestilence.

In the fifth seal we see the martyred souls of those who were beneath the throne, the many who will trust Jesus Christ during the first part of the Tribulation and who will be martyred for their faith and brought into the presence of God. They will accept Him too late to be included in the Bride of Christ.

In the sixth seal, as recorded in Revelation 6, God answers. Whether this answer comes immediately after the first five seals or whether it continues to the end of the time of the Great Tribulation, I am not certain. But during that time some terrible things will happen. A severe earthquake will occur; the sun will be darkened; the moon will become as blood; the stars will fall from Heaven; and the sky will be swept away like a scroll that is rolled up. Every mountain and island will be removed from its place. This is God's answer to man.

> The kings of the earth, and the great men, and the rich men, and the chief captains, and the mighty men, and every bondman, and every free man, hid themselves in the dens and in the rocks of the mountains; and said to the mountains and rocks, Fall on us, and hide us from the face of him that sitteth on the throne, and from the wrath of the lamb: for the great day of his wrath is come; and who shall be able to stand? (Rev. 6:15-17).

Between the sixth and seventh seal there is an interval of silence in Heaven.

> And when he had opened the seventh seal, there was silence in heaven about the space of half an hour (Rev. 8:1).

No doubt this silence came because everyone saw what was yet to come upon the earth. Possibly even the angels were frightened or awestricken because of the awfulness of the wrath to come upon men, the men who had defied and hated God, the men who had left Him out of their program and out of their plans, attempting to carry on in their own strength.

THE SEVEN TRUMPETS

When the seventh seal is opened, the seven trumpets are blown. These trumpets reveal the judgments which God allows Satan to bring upon man.

When the first trumpet is blown, hail and fire mingled with blood will fall upon the earth, burning one-third of the trees and the grass. In Job 2 we see how Satan operates.

When the second trumpet is blown, a burning mountain, probably a meteor, will fall into the sea and kill one-third of the sea life, wreck one-third of the ships, and cover one-third of the sea with the blood of those who are killed.

Then the third trumpet will blow, and a great star will fall, poisoning the streams and fresh water and causing death to all who drink thereof.

When the fourth trumpet blows, a third part of the sun, moon, and stars will be smitten and will thus lose one-third of their light. Further explanation of this trumpet is given in Luke 21:25, 26.

When the fifth trumpet blows, the angel will announce the first woe. The bottomless pit will be opened, and locusts will appear with the sting of a scorpion to torment ungodly men. This may be some form of demon possession.

And there came out of the smoke locusts upon the earth: and unto them was given power, as the scorpions of the earth have power. And it was commanded them that they should not hurt the grass of the earth, neither any green thing, neither any tree; but only those men which have not the seal of God in their foreheads. And to them it was given that they should not kill them, but that they should be tormented five months: and their torment was as the torment of a scorpion, when he striketh a man. And in those days shall men seek death, and shall not find it; and shall desire to die, and death shall flee from them (Rev. 9:3-6).

With the sixth trumpet comes the second woe. Four great angels appear at the head of a supernatural army of horsemen. The description of this is given in Revelation 9:13-21. They will slay one-third of the population of the earth with three plagues—the fire, the smoke, and the sulfur that will stream from their mouths. This is not the battle of Armageddon, if I understand the Scriptures correctly; rather, it is a terrible war which takes place after the great plague of demon possession. What an awful, awful time this will be!

The seventh trumpet announces the wrath of God, which will come when He pours out the seven vials of His wrath (Rev. 11:18, 19).

The Two Witnesses

At some time during the middle of this period God will send two witnesses to earth. We do not know exactly who these resurrected men are, for they are not mentioned by name. Many think that they might be Moses and Elijah. They will witness to the world and will preach the great Gospel of the kingdom, telling that the kingdom is about to come and warning men to repent and turn to God.

They will be protected by God as they witness for three and one-half years. Eventually the whole world will hear their message. The Antichrist and his forces will attempt in every way to kill them, but they will not be able to touch them until the three and one-half years are over.

Then suddenly these two witnesses will be slain. The people will be so happy that they are dead that they will celebrate. But after three and one-half days these two witnesses will suddenly arise and be taken into glory. Then great fear and trembling will come over all of the people of the earth. It is then that God prepares the way for His great wrath in the pouring out of the seven vials, the climax of which is the great battle of Armageddon.

THE UNHOLY TRINITY

During the Great Tribulation Satan will be embodied in the Antichrist, and the world will know who he is. He will break his covenant with Israel and attempt to destroy them. We find the description of this primarily in Revelation 12.

In Revelation 13 we read of another Beast, an Antispirit who will arise with power. An unholy trinity will then be seen—the Devil himself, the Antichrist, and the Antispirit. Much power will be given to them, for the Devil knows that his time is at hand.

Then God speaks in His final and great wrath.

THE SEVEN VIALS

We have already examined the seals, during which the wrath of man is revealed. At that time about one-fourth of the population of the earth will be destroyed. In the release of Satan's wrath in the trumpets one-third of the remaining population of the earth will be destroyed. This will leave approximately one-half of the population of the earth for the final wrath of God upon the earth, which will take place during the last half of the Tribulation period, or the Great Tribulation.

> And I heard a great voice out of the temple saying to the seven angels, Go your ways, and pour out the vials of the wrath of God upon the earth (Rev. 16:1).

This is God's Word. He has said that this will happen, and it will. Many have said that God will never pour out His wrath because He is only a God of love. Do not be deceived. God has said that if His love is spurned and rejected, His wrath will be seen, for God will vindicate His Son, who came all the way from Heaven to die for you. In the giving of His Son God manifested the greatest love that any human being can ever witness or receive. In turn His wrath will be just as great as His love has been.

There are seven vials of the wrath of God to be poured out. When the first vial is poured out, loathsome, painful sores will break out on men who have the mark of the beast.

When the second vial is poured out, the sea will become as blood, and every sea creature will perish.

The third vial shows that the rivers and fountains will become blood.

When the fourth vial is poured out, men will be scorched with the great heat. This makes them blaspheme God.

The fifth vial will be poured out, and darkness will come over the whole kingdom of the Beast. Men will gnaw their tongues because of the pain of the sores, which may have been caused by the terrible heat of the sun.

When the sixth vial is poured out, the Euphrates River will be dried up. Then the eastern kings will be able to cross in preparation for the battle of Armageddon.

The seventh vial will bring a great earthquake, followed by hailstones which will weigh as much as 100 pounds each. Many of these blasphemers will be killed.

THE FINAL DOOM

Then the final doom will come—a sevenfold doom—the doom upon the ecclesiastical system. The Church will be gone during the Tribulation, but the ecclesiastical system, the religious system, will remain. That system is here today, and it will stay here throughout the Tribulation. Many who have been denying the Word of God and the wrath of God and rejecting the love of God will find themselves under the wrath of God. But suddenly after the seven years of terrible Tribulation, God will bring an end to this ecclesiastical system with one great master stroke. The great commercial system on which so many are depending today will also come to an end. Even the political system will be abolished.

The Beast and the False Prophet, the Antichrist, will be cast alive into the great lake of fire. Finally even Satan will be cast into the bottomless pit, and there for one thousand years he will be imprisoned. At the end of the thousand years the lost will be brought into God's presence and judged. God does not give us all the details. He cannot because we could not understand them. Our finite minds cannot understand the greatness of God's love, the greatness of His work, or the terribleness of His wrath. But we have a picture which gives us a glimpse of the things to come.

A great invitation goes forth as all of these things come to a close and as the ecclesiastical system, the commercial system, the political system, the Beast, the False Prophet, the nations, and Satan are cast aside.

> I heard another voice from heaven, saying, Come out of her, my people, that ye be not partakers of her sins, and that ye receive not of her plagues (Rev. 18:4).

This is the voice that is now ringing forth. God has

opened the door of radio, the door of literature, and the door of the churches, that we might cry forth:

> Come out of her, my people, that ye be not partakers of her sins, and that ye receive not of her plagues. For her sins have reached unto heaven, and God hath remembered her iniquities (Rev. 18:4, 5).

We call out that same invitation today. We invite you to come to Jesus Christ, who died for your sin. In coming days men will cry for the rocks to fall upon them and for the mountains and the caves to hide them from the face of Him who will come in His great wrath. They will want a place to hide, but they will find none.

Jesus is the only hiding place. Only faith in His atoning blood will give you the safety and security of His protecting care. Come to Him now. Accept His loving forgiveness and escape the wrath and the judgment to come.

REWARDS

Norman H. Camp

Every man shall receive his own reward according to his own labor (I Cor. 3:8).

And, behold, I come quickly; and my reward is with me, to give every man according as his work shall be (Rev. 22:12).

REWARDS ARE GIVEN for faithful service. Parents reward their children, teachers reward their scholars, and masters reward their servants to encourage and stimulate them in their labors and to express appreciation of the work done. Sometimes rewards are promised in advance, and sometimes they are given as a surprise; but they are based upon the services rendered or the sacrifices made. The character of a reward generally depends upon the generosity and the ability of the one who bestows it.

Rewards differ from gifts. A gift is an expression of love and can never be claimed. A reward is bestowed because of labor performed and can always be claimed, if promised.

Salvation is a gift; it can never be merited. It is bestowed by grace upon those who confess themselves to be unworthy sinners and receive the Son of God as their personal Saviour. Salvation is not a reward for good works, as some seem to think. "For by grace [unmerited favor] are ye saved through faith; and that not of yourselves: it is the gift of God" (Eph. 2:8). But rewards are promised by God to those who are saved by grace, and

67

they are given according to the Christians' works after they are saved. We are not saved by good works, but we are saved unto good works, "which God hath before ordained that we should walk in them" (Eph. 2:10). Good works are an evidence of saving faith and the fruit of saving faith, just as the fruit of an apple tree is evidence that there is life in the tree. The apples do not produce the life of the tree, but the life of the tree produces the apples.

Rewards are not gifts. A gift may be given or bestowed, but a reward must be merited in some way. It may be a prophet's reward for receiving a prophet, or a righteous man's reward for receiving a righteous man, or a reward for giving a cup of cold water to some little one, or a great reward for suffering persecution for Jesus' sake, or a full reward for walking in the truth to the end. (See Matt. 5:12; 10:41, 42; II John 8.)

Rewards are similar to wages and, therefore, are received as a result of the work done or the deeds performed. The difference between rewards and wages is that wages are the direct result of the deeds done and are usually received in this life, while rewards are generally bestowed in the future in recognition of the work done. For example, we read that "the wages of sin is death" (Rom. 6:23), and "he that soweth to his flesh shall of the flesh reap corruption" (Gal. 6:8). These are some of the wages received in this life.

On the other hand, the Christian is told to do all things heartily as unto the Lord, "knowing that of the Lord ye shall receive the reward of the inheritance" (Col. 3:24). In I Peter 1:4 we are told that this inheritance is "incorruptible, and undefiled, and that fadeth not away, reserved in heaven for you, who are kept by the power of God."

There are rewards for evil works as well as for good works. Everyone reaps what he sows. This is clearly revealed in experience and is taught in the Bible. It is written of the wicked: "Woe unto the wicked! it shall be ill with him: for the reward of his hands shall be given him" (Isa. 3:11). "As thou hast done, it shall be done unto thee: thy reward shall return upon thine own head" (Obad. 15). "Be not deceived; God is not mocked: for whatsoever a man soweth, that shall he also reap" (Gal. 6:7). The ungodly "shall receive the reward of unrighteousness" (II Peter 2:13). This is a fixed rule in both the natural and the spiritual life.

On the other hand, the righteous receive their reward. As it is written: "Verily there is a reward for the righteous" (Ps. 58:11). "To him that soweth righteousness shall be a sure reward" (Prov. 11:18). "The reward of humility and the fear of Jehovah is riches, and honor, and life" (Prov. 22:4, A.R.V.). Of the Lord Jesus Christ it is written: "Thou hast loved righteousness, and hated iniquity; therefore God, even thy God, hath anointed thee with the oil of gladness above all thy fellows" (Heb. 1:9). This was His reward.

Some rewards are received during this life, and some will be received in the life to come. Jesus spoke of those who give their alms to be seen of men and who pray long prayers in public to be heard of men. Then He added, "Verily I say unto you, They have their reward" (Matt. 6:2).

The reward which they receive now is the praise of men. There are those who love the praise of men more than the praise of God (John 12:43) and, therefore, will not confess Jesus Christ as Saviour and Lord. On the other hand, those who give and pray in secret are seen by God and will later be rewarded openly by Him. (Read Matt. 6:1-21.)

Future Rewards

Although some rewards are received in this life, most of them are bestowed by God in the future. This is necessarily so, because the entire life and the whole work performed must be taken into account in the bestowal of the reward. There are many factors which enter into the nature of the reward. Many things must be considered. The motives for doing the work, as well as the work done, must be taken into account. God alone is able to weigh all of the factors involved and render a fair decision. This decision must be fair not only from God's but also from man's viewpoint; therefore, the one making the decision must be both God and man. There is only One who can meet this requirement, and He is Christ Jesus—the God-Man—God manifested in the flesh. He is the One who will judge the world and will reward every man according to his works (Acts 17:31; John 5:22, 23; Matt. 16:27). This is promised in the Old Testament and confirmed in the New Testament.

In Isaiah 40:10 (R.V.) we read, "Behold, the Lord Jehovah will come as a mighty one, and his arm will rule for him: behold, his reward is with him, and his recompense before him." Since the "Jehovah" of the Old Testament is the "Jesus" of the New Testament, it was perfectly proper for Jesus to say: "For the Son of man shall come in the glory of his Father with his angels; and then he shall reward every man according to his works" (Matt. 16:27). "Behold, I come quickly; and my reward is with me, to give every man according as his work shall be" (Rev. 22:12). At that time "every man shall receive his own reward according to his own labor" (I Cor. 3:8).

These rewards are for God's born-again people who are faithful in service, steadfast in faith, and victorious in life over the world, the flesh, and the Devil. There are some Christians who will not receive a reward, because their works will not stand the acid test. Their works will be like wood, hay, and stubble, to be burned up; and these Christians will be saved "so as by fire" (I Cor. 3:10-15). There are other Christians who will lose part of their reward because they have not been watchful (II John 8). But there are those Christians who will receive a full reward, consisting of one or more crowns, and will have an abundant entrance into the everlasting kingdom of Christ (II Peter 1:10, 11).

The Christian's Crowns

There are five crowns mentioned in Scripture which are promised to God's children upon certain conditions. They may be won or they may be lost (Rev. 3:11). They are spoken of as prizes (I Cor. 9:24; Phil. 3:13, 14). They are described as crowns of gold (Rev. 4:4).

1. *The Incorruptible Crown* (I Cor. 9:25). This crown is given to those who are temperate in all things and who are not indulging the appetites of the body, in order that they may faithfully preach the Gospel to all men, whether Jew or Gentile, whereby at least some shall be saved (vv. 16-27).

2. *The Crown of Rejoicing* (I Thess. 2:19). This crown is given to those who win souls for Christ, whether by personal work, by preaching the Gospel, or by distributing the Gospel in print. Solomon declared, "He that winneth souls is wise" (Prov. 11:30), and Daniel said that "they that be wise shall shine as the brightness of the firmament; and they that turn many to righteousness as the stars for ever and ever" (Dan. 12:3). Every soul saved through the prayers and efforts of the servant of Christ will be a part of his crown of rejoicing when he stands before the Judgment Seat of Christ and is rewarded according to his labors.

3. *The Crown of Glory* (I Peter 5:4). This is the crown which is given to faithful pastors who have willingly cared for the flock of God as overseers—not as lords and not for the sake of financial gain, but as a shepherd who cares for his sheep. Such pastors practice what they preach and are examples to others. They feed the flock with the Word of God—"rightly dividing the word of truth," so that they will grow in grace and become fruitful in their lives and labors. They warn the flock against false teachers and the prevalent errors of the day, encouraging them to contend earnestly for the faith (Jude 3, 4). All such pastors and teachers will receive a crown of glory which will not tarnish or fade away.

4. *The Crown of Righteousness* (II Tim. 4:8). This crown is given to all those who love the appearing of Christ. They not only are trusting Christ for salvation and loving Him because He loved them, but they are also looking forward to the personal coming of Christ in glory and power, when they will be caught up with other Christians in the clouds to meet Him in the air (I Thess. 4:14-17). Because of this blessed hope, they endure afflictions, fight the good fight of faith, and speak the truth in love. They are loyal and faithful to Christ at all times, for they know not when He may appear for His own. All such are to receive a special crown.

5. *The Crown of Life* (James 1:12; Rev. 2:10). This crown is given to all who endure trials and temptations even unto death for Jesus' sake. "They loved not their lives unto the death" (Rev. 12:11). Many of those who receive this crown, such as Stephen, James, John, Peter, Paul, Huss, Tyndale, Latimer, Cranmer, and many others, are martyrs for the sake of Christ. (Read Foxe's *Book of Martyrs.*)

The crown of life is to be distinguished from the gift of life, which is mentioned in John 4:10; John 5:24;

Romans 6:23; and Ephesians 2:8. Eternal life is a free gift from God to all who believe on His Son. "He that hath the Son hath life" (I John 5:11, 12). But those who receive eternal life through faith in Christ may also receive the crown of life in addition, if so be that they suffer for Him even unto death.

Those of recent years who will receive the crown of life are the Christians in China who were massacred for their faith during the Boxer's uprising in 1900 and the Armenian Christians who were massacred by the Turks during World War I. During the coming Great Tribulation many will receive the crown of life because they will be slain for the Word of God and for the testimony which they hold (Rev. 6:9-11).

OTHER REWARDS

In addition to these crowns there are certain rewards promised to overcoming Christians, as is recorded in chapters 2 and 3 of Revelation. Some will be given a white stone with a new name written thereon; some will be given authority over the nations and will rule them with a rod of iron; others will be arrayed in white raiment; and still others will be granted the right to sit with Christ on His throne. All of these rewards will far surpass anything that man can imagine.

Christians are admonished by the apostle John, who had a glimpse of the coming glory and kingdom of God, "Look to yourselves, that we lose not those things which we have wrought, but that we receive a full reward" (II John 8); and also by the risen Christ, "Behold, I come quickly: hold that fast which thou hast, that no man take thy crown" (Rev. 3:11).

This is the divine order if a Christian is to receive a reward: (1) Make sure of your own personal salvation (II Cor. 13:5; II Peter 1:10). (2) "Work out your own sal-

vation with fear and trembling; for it is God which work-
eth in you" (Phil. 2:12, 13; II Peter 1:5-8). (3) Reach forward to the things which are before (it is better farther
on) and "press toward the mark for the prize of the high
calling of God in Christ Jesus" (Phil. 3:13, 14; I Cor. 9:24).
(4) Use the talents which God has given you, whether they
be many or few, and do not be weary in well-doing (Matt.
25:14-30; Luke 19:11-26; Gal. 6:9).

(Reprinted from *Thinking with God,* by Norman H.
Camp, by permission of Moody Press, 820 N. La Salle,
Chicago, Illinois)

HOW WILL CHRIST JUDGE
THE NATIONS?

William L. Pettingill

God . . . now commandeth all men everywhere to repent: because he hath appointed a day, in the which he will judge the world in righteousness by that man whom he hath ordained; whereof he hath given assurance unto all men, in that he hath raised him from the dead (Acts 17:30, 31).

THUS SPOKE THE APOSTLE to the Gentiles in his first proclamation of the Gospel in the great Gentile city of Athens.

This word concerning judgment may include, at least in principle, all judgment. The whole world, embracing all human beings who ever have lived and all who ever will live, must sooner or later face the Son of God in judgment, except those who have taken their place under the sheltering blood of the covenant. These have already passed from death unto life and will not come into judgment (John 5:24). For the rest, who have persisted in turning from God's offered salvation in grace, nothing remains "but a certain fearful looking for of judgment and fiery indignation, which shall devour the adversaries" (Heb. 10:27).

THE FATE OF THE HEATHEN

If someone asks how this affects the case of the heathen world which has not heard the Gospel, the answer is that "they are without excuse" who refuse to worship God (Rom. 1:20). The Judge of all the earth knows how to do right (Gen. 18:25), and He knows how to measure responsibility. Therefore, we must leave the heathen world to His righteous judgment. But let us see to it that no part of the heathen world is left in ignorance of the Gospel through any fault of ours. Our Lord Jesus Christ has plainly marked out our task, and we are to be His witnesses "unto the uttermost part of the earth" (Acts 1:8). "He is the propitiation . . . for the sins of the whole world" (I John 2:2), and we must carry the good news to every creature. As someone has said, "The question is not so much what God will do with the heathen who have not heard the Gospel, as what God will do with us if we fail to send the Gospel to the heathen." The Son of God is "the Saviour of the world" (John 4:42), and it is a tragedy that the greater part of the world has never heard of Him. Whose fault is that?

But the Lord Jesus is not only the Saviour; He is also the Judge of all the earth.

> For the Father judgeth no man, but hath committed all judgment unto the Son: that all men should honor the Son, even as they honor the Father . . . For as the Father hath life in himself; so hath he given to the Son to have life in himself; and hath given him authority to execute judgment also, because he is the Son of man (John 5:22-27).

Let us avoid confusing the judgment of the nations with the judgment of the lost dead, described in Revelation 20:11-15. Both of these accounts are often headlined, "The Last and General Judgment," but there is no such thing as a "general judgment" spoken of in Scripture. The judgment of the lost dead follows the Millennium, but the judgment of the living nations precedes the Millennium. A comparison of Matthew 25:31-46 with Revelation 20:11-15 will reveal many contrasts. In the later judgment there is a resurrection, and books are opened; in the earlier judgment these features are absent. Let us examine the judgment of living nations, as described in Matthew 25:31-46:

> When the Son of man shall come in his glory, and all the holy angels with him, then shall he sit upon the throne of his glory: and before him shall be gathered all nations: and he shall separate them one from another, as a shepherd divideth his sheep from the goats: and he shall set the sheep on his right hand, but the goats on the left. Then shall the King say unto them on his right hand, Come, ye blessed of my Father, inherit the kingdom prepared for you from the foundation of the world: for I was an hungred, and ye gave me meat: I was thirsty, and ye gave me drink: I was a stranger, and ye took me in: naked, and ye clothed me: I was sick, and ye visited me: I was in prison, and ye came unto me. Then shall the righteous answer him, saying, Lord, when saw we thee an hungred, and fed thee? or thirsty, and gave thee drink? When saw we thee a stranger, and took thee in? or naked, and clothed thee? Or when saw we thee sick, or in prison, and came unto thee? And the king shall answer and say unto them, Verily, I say unto you, Inasmuch as ye have done it unto one of the least of these my brethren, ye have done it unto me. Then shall he say also unto them on the left hand, Depart from me, ye cursed, into everlasting fire, prepared for the devil and his angels: for I was an hungred, and ye gave me no meat: I was thirsty, and ye gave me no drink: I was a stranger, and ye took me not in: naked, and ye clothed me not: sick, and in prison, and ye visited me not. Then shall they also answer him, saying, Lord, when saw we thee an hungred, or athirst, or a stranger, or naked, or sick, or in prison, and did not minister unto thee? Then shall he answer them, saying, Verily I say unto you, Inasmuch as ye did it not to one of the least of these, ye did it not to me.

And these shall go away into everlasting punishment: but the righteous into life eternal.

The Time of the Judgment

The time of the judgment is determined by the words *when* and *then* in Matthew 25:31. It will be at the time "when the Son of man shall come in his glory," at the end of the age. The seventieth week of Daniel will by that time have run its course. The Church, the Body of Christ, will have been "present with the Lord" for seven full years. The terrible scenes of the Great Tribulation will have come to an end with the battle of Armageddon, and the Lord Jesus will have been "revealed from heaven with his mighty angels" (II Thess. 1:7). "Then shall he sit upon the throne of his glory" (Matt. 25:31). He has come to "judge and make war" (Rev. 19:11). Revealed from Heaven "in flaming fire," He comes to take "vengeance on them that know not God, and that obey not the gospel of our Lord Jesus Christ" (II Thess. 1:8).

The Place of the Judgment

The location is indicated in Joel's account of this judgment of nations.

> I will also gather all nations, and will bring them down into the valley of Jehoshaphat . . . Let the heathen be wakened, and come up to the valley of Jehoshaphat: for there will I sit to judge all the heathen round about (Joel 3:1, 12).

The Subjects of the Judgment

In the Joel passage the word *goiim* is translated "nations" in verse 2 and "heathen" twice in verse 12. In both Joel and Matthew it is equivalent to "Gentiles." This is distinctly a judgment of Gentiles. Arraigned before the throne of glory will be those Gentile peoples who are found living upon the earth at the second advent of Christ to the earth. If it be objected that the valley of Jehoshaphat could not contain all these Gentiles at once, it is sufficient to answer that they may not all be there at once. They must, however, pass in review before that throne and be divided by the Son of Man upon the throne, "as a shepherd divideth his sheep from the goats: and he shall set the sheep on his right hand, but the goats on the left."

The Tests of the Judgment

The basis of the judgment by which the Gentiles will be tested is their treatment of a third group whom the King called "my brethren." These, as will be seen in Joel's account, are Jews. Doubtlessly they are those Jews who will have turned to the Lord after the catching away of the Church. Immediately upon their conversion this Jewish remnant becomes God's evangelizing agency and begins the work of proclaiming the King's approaching advent "in the clouds of heaven with power and great glory" (Matt. 24:30). "And [at this time] this gospel of the kingdom shall be preached in all the world for a witness unto all nations [Gentiles]; and then shall the end come" (Matt. 24:14). "I will send those that escape of them unto the nations . . . that have not heard my fame, neither have seen my glory; and they shall declare my glory among the Gentiles" (Isa. 66:19).

The King on the throne identifies himself with these Jewish evangelizers, His "brethren," His "kinsmen according to the flesh" (Rom. 9:3). The "sheep" on the right hand are commended for ministering to Him, and the "goats" on the left hand are condemned for failure to do so. The "sheep" have believed the Gospel of the kingdom and have, therefore, received and harbored those who preached it to them. The "goats" have rejected the message and have, therefore, turned from the messengers. Both classes are surprised to learn that in thus dealing with the Jewish remnant they have been dealing with the King himself. The same principle was revealed to Saul of Tarsus on the Damascus highway. He thought that he had been serving God in persecuting the Christians, but he learned that all the time he had been persecuting the Lord Jesus Himself. "Saul, Saul, why persecutest thou me?" In all our afflictions He is afflicted.

In Joel 3 we read:

> For, behold, in those days, and in that time, when I shall bring again the captivity of Judah and Jerusalem, I will also gather all nations, and will bring them down into the valley of Jehoshaphat, and will plead with them there for my people and for my heritage Israel, whom they have scattered among the nations, and parted my land. And they have cast lots for my people, and have given a boy for an harlot, and sold a girl for wine, that they might drink. Yea, and what have ye to do with me, O Tyre, and Zidon, and all the coasts of Palestine? will ye render me a recompense? and if ye recompense me, swiftly and speedily will I return your recompense upon your own head; because ye have taken my silver and my gold, and have carried into your temples my goodly pleasant things: the children also of Judah and the children of Jerusalem have ye sold unto the Grecians, that ye might remove them far from their border. Behold, I will raise them out of the place whither ye have sold them, and will return your recompense upon your own head: and I will sell your sons and your daughters into the hand of the children of Judah, and they shall sell them to the Sabeans, to a people far off: for the Lord hath spoken it. Proclaim ye this among the Gentiles; Prepare war, wake up the mighty men, let all the men of war draw near; let them come up: beat your plowshares into swords, and your pruninghooks into spears: let the weak

say, I am strong. Assemble yourselves, and come, all ye heathen, and gather yourselves together round about: thither cause thy mighty ones to come down, O Lord. Let the heathen be wakened, and come up to the valley of Jehoshaphat: for there will I sit to judge all the heathen round about. Put ye in the sickle, for the harvest is ripe: come, get you down; for the press is full, the fats overflow; for their wickedness is great. Multitudes, multitudes in the valley of decision: for the day of the Lord is near in the valley of decision. The sun and the moon shall be darkened, and the stars shall withdraw their shining. The Lord also shall roar out of Zion, and utter his voice from Jerusalem; and the heavens and the earth shall shake: but the Lord will be the hope of his people, and the strength of the children of Israel. So shall ye know that I am the Lord your God dwelling in Zion, my holy mountain: then shall Jerusalem be holy, and there shall no stranger pass through her any more. And it shall come to pass in that day, that the mountains shall drop down new wine, and the hills shall flow with milk, and all the rivers of Judah shall flow with waters, and a fountain shall come forth of the house of the Lord, and shall water the valley of Shittim.

The correspondence between this passage and that of Matthew 25 is very striking. The Gentiles have much to be settled because of their treatment of the Jews, and this settlement must be made with the Man now sitting at God's right hand "when he shall come to be glorified in his saints, and to be admired in all them that believe" (II Thess. 1:10).

The Result of Judgment

This is summed up briefly in Matthew 25:46:

And these shall go away into everlasting punishment: but the righteous into life eternal.

The adjective is the same in both clauses of the sentence. The punishment is *aionian,* and the life is *aionian.* Both are endless. There is endless punishment for those on the left hand and endless life for those on the right hand. Many efforts have been made to tone down the endless punishment, but there it stands together with the endless life. Both are *aionian,* everlasting, eternal, endless. Let no one trifle with this solemn declaration, "for the mouth of the Lord hath spoken it."

(Reprinted from *God's Prophecies for Plain People,* by William L. Pettingill, by permission of Van Kampen Press, Wheaton, Illinois)

THE MILLENNIUM

C. I. Scofield

WE ARE TO LOOK now at the teachings of the Scriptures concerning the Millennium. The word signifies a period of one thousand years. The term itself means no more than that, and it is derived from the measure of time given to this period in Revelation 20:1-6.

In this passage we find a period of one thousand years mentioned four times. This period coincides in prophetic order with the time of blessedness on this earth under the personal reign of Messiah, long ago foretold by the Old Testament prophets.

It is to be regretted, however, that this word *millennium* ever supplanted the old Biblical word *kingdom*. Many misconceptions in people's minds might, perhaps, never have been there if we had always referred to this period as the kingdom period, the time when the kingdom of Heaven will have its manifestation.

No doubt when most of us pray, "Thy kingdom come," we really have in mind the wish that more people may be converted. Some perhaps mean the bringing in of that time of which we have been told (but not by Scripture) when all the people in the world will be members of the Church. Scripture never speaks of a time in this age when the whole world would be a converted world. Only in the kingdom age will every intelligence be subject to God, and that is what our Lord had in mind when He told us to pray, "Thy kingdom come." He referred to the kingdom foretold by the prophets, the time when the earth "shall be full of the knowledge of the Lord."

Remember that the Scriptures always distinguish between the Church and the kingdom. Let me rapidly give some distinctions which you yourself may verify by recourse to your Bible.

In the first place, we have in Scripture the expression "the kingdom of God," and we may say that this expression gives its own definition. It includes whatever God rules over, the intelligences in any world or in any sphere who are willingly subject to the rule of God. If there are intelligent beings in the most distant star who submit themselves to the rule and will of God, there the kingdom of God is established; there the kingdom of God exists.

Secondly, "the kingdom of heaven" is mentioned in Scripture. That is a more limited term; it refers to this period which we call the Millennium. The "kingdom of God" is a great inclusive expression that takes in the whole sphere which God rules. The "kingdom of heaven" is the establishment, through Christ, of God's righteous reign on the earth. It is always limited to the earth; that is its sphere, even though glorified saints of this age and past ages are concerned with it.

Thirdly, we have the Church. The Church is composed of those who are saved, mostly Gentiles, between the first and second advent of the Lord Jesus Christ. More strictly speaking, it is between the Day of Pentecost and that day when "the Lord himself shall descend from heaven with a shout, with the voice of the archangel, and with the trump of God: and the dead in Christ shall rise first: then we which are alive and remain shall be caught up together with them in the clouds, to meet the Lord in the air" (I Thess. 4:16, 17). Between those two points, the Day of Pentecost and the descent of the Lord in the air for the saints of this dispensation, the Church is being formed.

The apostle Paul said, you remember, that the Church was a mystery that was hidden from the Old Testament writers. To him was given the unfolding of that mystery, and he tells us that the Church is the Body of Christ and the Bride of Christ. The saints who compose it are kings and priests, and to them is reserved the unique distinction of reigning with Christ "over the earth."

> Thou wast slain, and hast redeemed us to God by thy blood out of every kindred, and tongue, and people, and nation; and hast made us unto our God kings and priests: and we shall reign over the earth (Rev. 5:9, 10).

Notice that there is a limitation of the reigning of the saints. We shall not reign in Heaven; we shall not reign in that wide sphere which is called the kingdom of God, but we shall reign over the earth.

These distinctions are fundamental to any clear understanding of the Scriptures. The kingdom of God is the great inclusive term. The kingdom of Heaven has its full manifestation in the thousand-year reign of Christ over the earth. The Church is a distinct body of those who were saved between Pentecost and the descent of the Lord into the air just before the Tribulation; these will be associated with Him in the rule when the kingdom of Heaven is set up.

The kingdom of Heaven is in the kingdom of God, but the two terms are not synonymous. For example, the State of Texas is in the United States, but it is not the United States. Because it is in the United States it has much in common with the United States. It has the same president; the same constitution is the supreme law; the same language is spoken; but it would be mere confusion to speak of the State of Texas and the United States interchangeably. The kingdom of Scotland is in Great Britain, but it is not Great Britain.

The kingdom of Heaven is in the kingdom of God. Therefore, we may expect to find in the Scriptures many things which are characteristic of the kingdom of God but which are not necessarily applicable to the kingdom of Heaven.

The Church is in the kingdom of God, but the Church is not the kingdom of God, neither is the Church the kingdom of Heaven, although for a time the Church is to be in the kingdom of Heaven. The Church is in the kingdom of Heaven, which is in the kingdom of God, just as the royal family of Great Britain, for instance, may be said to be in the kingdom of Great Britain. The Church is a body of royal priests called out during this dispensation to be co-rulers with the King over the millennial earth during a period of one thousand years and to be forever with Him after that period is ended.

THE TIME OF THE MILLENNIUM

First of all, when does the Millennium begin? It begins immediately after the Great Tribulation has run its course. Immediately after the Great Tribulation the Lord Jesus returns in power and glory to this earth and sets up the millennial kingdom. Let us read one or two passages upon that point.

Immediately after the tribulation of those days shall the sun be darkened, and the moon shall not give her light, and the stars shall fall from heaven, and the powers of the heavens shall be shaken: and then shall appear the sign of the Son of man in heaven: and then shall all the tribes of the earth mourn, and they shall see the Son of man coming in the clouds of heaven with power and great glory (Matt. 24:29, 30).

When? "Immediately after the tribulation of those days."

You perceive the distinction between this coming of the Lord in power and great glory to the earth after the period called the Great Tribulation and that other coming of the Lord into the air to take away His own before the Tribulation. That coming which precedes the Tribulation is visible only to those who are caught up to meet the Lord in the air. It will be known to the dwellers on the earth only by the absence of those who have been taken. The other coming will be "as the lightning cometh out of the east, and shineth even unto the west." It will be witnessed by all tongues and nations, and for them it will be an awful event. That is clearly established by the words of the Lord Himself.

THE ORDER OF EVENTS

In the second place, let us trace from Scripture the order of events in the establishment of this millennial kingdom.

Here I shall confine myself almost entirely to the inspired words, and I am sure that I need make no apology for reading upon such a subject as this exclusively from Scripture. It would be mere impertinence for me or any other man to ask his fellow mortals to hear his own theories about the future. We do not know what may occur one hour hence except for what God has revealed. To Scripture, then, we turn to learn how the Millennium will be introduced.

And I saw heaven opened, and behold a white horse; and he that sat upon him was called Faithful and True, and in righteousness he doth judge and make war. His eyes were as a flame of fire, and on his head were many crowns; and he had a name written, that no one knew, but he himself. And he was clothed with a vesture

dipped in blood: and his name is called the Word of God
(Rev. 19:11-13).

Who is this personage?

In the first chapter of the Gospel of John we have
this name, "the Word," applied to the Lord Jesus Christ,
the eternal Son of God. "In the beginning was the Word,
and the Word was with God, and the Word was God." A
little later we read: "And the Word was made flesh, and
dwelt among us, and we beheld his glory."

Where is Jesus now? He is in Heaven at the right
hand of the Father. In this passage we see prophetically,
through the vision of the apocalyptic seer, the moment
when Heaven is opened; and Jesus Christ, "the Word,"
issues forth, not now to become the babe of Bethlehem,
but the man of Calvary, armed as for war, "his vesture
dipped in blood."

Next the prophets describe the arrival of the Lord
Jesus with the armies of Heaven upon the earth (Rev.
19:14). This is the time when the seventieth week of
Daniel, the Great Tribulation, ends. The host of the
Beast and False Prophet will be gathered against the
Jewish remnant in Jerusalem.

> Proclaim ye this among the Gentiles; Prepare war,
> wake up the mighty men, let all the men of war draw
> near; let them come up: beat your plowshares into
> swords, and your pruninghooks into spears . . . Assem-
> ble yourselves, and come, all ye heathen, and gather
> yourselves together round about (Joel 3:9-11).
>
> For I will gather all nations against Jerusalem to
> battle (Zech. 14:2).
>
> And I saw the beast, and the kings of the earth, and
> their armies, gathered together to make war against him
> that sat on the horse, and against his army (Rev. 19:19).

Just at this crisis the Lord appears in glory and
delivers the beleaguered Jewish saints.

I beheld, and the same horn made war with the saints,
and prevailed against them; until the Ancient of days
came (Dan. 7:21, 22).

Then shall the Lord go forth, and fight against those
nations, as when he fought in the day of battle. And his
feet shall stand in that day upon the Mount of Olives,
which is before Jerusalem on the east . . . And the Lord
shall be king over all the earth (Zech. 14:3, 4, 9).

And the beast was taken [slain], and with him the
false prophet that wrought miracles before him, with
which he deceived them that had received the mark of
the beast, and them that worshiped his image (Rev.
19:20).

And I saw an angel come down from heaven, having
the key of the bottomless pit and a great chain in his
hand. And he laid hold on the dragon, that old serpent,
which is the Devil, and Satan, and bound him a thousand years (Rev. 20:1, 2).

Now keep the connection. In the vision of John on the
Isle of Patmos we have seen Heaven opened and the Lord
descending with His mighty ones to the earth. He comes
at a time of crisis on the earth, when the saints who have
turned to Him during the Tribulation are at their utmost
extremity, and He delivers them. He wins the great final
victory.

The next act in the mighty drama is the final regathering of dispersed Israel. A remnant has been in the land
through the Tribulation, but now the nation is to be
brought back. Observe how this follows the coming of
the King:

Behold, the days come, saith the Lord, that I will
raise unto David a righteous Branch, and a King shall
reign and prosper, and shall execute judgment and
justice in the earth (Jer. 23:5).

This is not a question of the reigning of God in
Heaven. His throne is in the heavens, and it has never

been shaken and never can be; but here we have the promise that David's great Son will be One who will reign and execute judgment and justice on the earth. Did He do anything of that kind when He came before? Did He reign in prosperity? It is said that He was crucified through weakness and that He had "not where to lay his head." Even the fowls of the air and the foxes of the earth were better off than He. Was there any fulfillment of this promise then? Do you not see that the fulfillment of this prediction requires the return of David's Son to this earth?

The Judgment of the Nations

In Matthew 25:31-34 we have the next event in order:

> When the Son of man shall come in his glory, and all the holy angels with him, then shall he sit upon the throne of his glory: and before him shall be gathered all nations: and he shall separate them one from another, as a shepherd divideth his sheep from the goats: and he shall set the sheep on his right hand, but the goats on the left. Then shall the King say unto them on his right hand, Come, ye blessed of my Father, inherit the kingdom prepared for you from the foundation of the world.

The group on His right hand forms the Gentile nucleus of the population of the millennial earth. Those upon His left hand go away into eternal punishment. The basis of judgment is the treatment that they have accorded His "brethren," the believing Jewish remnant, during the Tribulation just ended.

I am aware that the judgment of Matthew 25, the judgment that our Lord declares to be the judgment of the nations, has been confounded in the minds of many with the judgment of the Great White Throne, as recorded in Revelation 20. But surely no one needs to be confused. Note, first, the difference in time of the two judgments.

The judgment of the living nations takes place when Christ comes in glory. The judgment of the Great White Throne takes place after a thousand years of His presence on the earth. Note also that in the judgment of the Great White Throne only "the dead" are raised and stand before God. In the judgment of Matthew 25 there is no resurrection at all. It is simply a judgment of the nations.

It should ever be borne in mind that these prophecies deal with the nations of Christendom, to whom the Gospel has gone.

What follows? "In his days Judah shall be saved, and Israel shall dwell safely" (Jer. 23:6).

Did that happen when the Lord was here before? On the contrary, we know that almost immediately after His final rejection and crucifixion the Roman armies came up to Jerusalem, destroyed the city, together with nearly half of the inhabitants, and carried the remainder into captivity. Nothing in all the calamitous history of this wonderful city was so terrible as the destruction of Jerusalem by Titus. But read Jeremiah 23:7, 8:

> Therefore, behold, the days come, saith the Lord, that they shall no more say, The Lord liveth, which brought up the children of Israel out of the land of Egypt; but, The Lord liveth, which brought up and which led the seed of the house of Israel out of the north country, and from all countries whither I had driven them; and they shall dwell in their own land.

Is not that explicit enough? Has that ever been fulfilled? A remnant of the Jews are to be in the land during the Great Tribulation, and they will turn to the Lord Jesus as their Messiah. He will come back, first of all, for their deliverance and then for the judgment of the Gentiles according to their treatment of Israel.

It is such a wonderful regathering!

> They shall no more say, The Lord liveth, which brought up the children of Israel out of the land of Egypt.

That was a wonderful deliverance. An old shepherd, an eighty-year-old Jewish man, brought millions of slaves out from under the power of the mightiest monarch of those times without a soldier or a spear, with just a shepherd's staff. The waters of the Red Sea were divided, and Israel passed through and into the wilderness dry-shod. Then forty years later the waters of the Jordan were parted, and the Israelites passed into their own land dry-shod. I repeat that these were wonderful deliverances; yet the coming deliverance of Israel will be so much greater and so much more marvelous that the wonders of the first exodus and deliverance will be forgotten.

In "the wilderness of the people" Jesus meets them, and they receive Him as the Christ.

That introduces the Millennium.

Millions of souls now living have never heard the Gospel. To them, or to those who may at that time be unevangelized, Israel becomes a missionary nation.

> And it shall come to pass, that as ye were a curse among the heathen, O house of Judah, and house of Israel; so will I save you, and ye shall be a blessing . . . Yea, many people and strong nations shall come to seek the Lord of hosts in Jerusalem, and to pray before the Lord. Thus saith the Lord of hosts; In those days it shall come to pass, that ten men shall take hold out of all languages of the nations, even shall take hold of the skirt of him that is a Jew, saying, We will go with you: for we have heard that God is with you (Zech. 8:13, 22, 23).

At last there will be a converted world; but it is in the kingdom of Heaven, not in the period of the Church.

THE FORM OF GOVERNMENT

What will be the form of government and the order of society during the Millennium?

The government will be a theocracy. God Himself will rule over the earth in the person of Jesus Christ, the Son of David.

> Behold, the days come, saith the Lord, that I will raise unto David a righteous Branch, and a King shall reign and prosper, and shall execute judgment and justice in the earth (Jer. 23:5).

> And the angel said unto her, Fear not, Mary: for thou hast found favor with God. And, behold, thou shalt conceive in thy womb, and bring forth a son, and shalt call his name Jesus. He shall be great, and shall be called the Son of the Highest: and the Lord God shall give unto him the throne of his father David: and he shall reign over the house of Jacob forever (Luke 1:30-33).

Where will be the seat of that government? Let us read from Isaiah 2. "The word that Isaiah the son of Amoz saw concerning Judah and Jerusalem" (v. 1). (The word was not concerning Washington, London, Paris, Vienna, or Berlin, but concerning Judah and Jerusalem. Let us take it for granted that the Spirit of God knew how to dictate His messages.)

> And it shall come to pass in the last days, that the mountain of the Lord's house shall be established in the top of the mountains, and shall be exalted above the hills; and all nations shall flow unto it. And many people shall go and say, Come ye, and let us go up to the mountain of the Lord, to the house of the God of Jacob; and he will teach us of his ways, and we will walk in his paths: for out of Zion shall go forth the law, and the word of the Lord from Jerusalem. And he shall judge among the nations, and shall rebuke many people: and they shall beat their swords into plowshares, and their spears into pruninghooks: nation shall not lift up sword

against nation, neither shall they learn war any more
(Isa. 2:2-4).

Jerusalem is to be the seat of the government.

Israel will have the first place among nations during
the Millennium. At the present time the nations are a
headless body—there is no chief nation. If we pointed
out one nation as the head, our claim would instantly be
contested. Today the whole sphere of the Gentile world
is divided, localized, with no nation at the head; and
there never will be any nation at the head again until
Israel is the head. Proof of that is found in the writings
of the prophets.

Concerning Israel God said:

> And I will restore thy judges as at first, and thy coun-
> selors as at the beginning: afterward thou shalt be called,
> The city of righteousness, the faithful city (Isa. 1:26).

To the apostles He said:

> When the Son of man shall sit in the throne of his
> glory, ye also shall sit upon twelve thrones, judging the
> twelve tribes of Israel (Matt. 19:28).

The office of judge in Israel was not a judicial office,
but an administrative office.

Concerning the manner of governing during the Millennium, we gather a hint from Luke 19. We read that a
certain nobleman goes into a far country to receive a kingdom. After a long time the nobleman, having received the
kingdom, returns and reckons with his servants. To one
who had received one pound and had gained ten pounds,
the king said, "Well, thou faithful servant . . . have thou
authority over ten cities." Do you understand? Where is
this authority to be exercised? Will it be in Heaven? Are
there many cities in Heaven? No, Heaven is one city.
This could not be any place except on the earth.

In Hebrews we find the distinct statement that "unto the angels hath he not put in subjection the world [or age] to come," but unto us. We have, in short, this thought: The administration of the kingly authority of Christ over the earth during the Millennium is through restoration of the administrative office of judge over Israel and through the personal service of saints in their glorified bodies over the Gentiles; the heavens and the earth, so to speak, come together during that period of one thousand years.

The Condition of the Earth

What will be the condition of the earth during that period?

When the prophets paint the picture of the millennial earth, they dip their pens in the rainbow. Their descriptions are incomparably beautiful.

> And there shall come forth a rod out of the stem of Jesse, and a Branch shall grow out of his roots: and the spirit of the Lord shall rest upon him, the spirit of wisdom and understanding, the spirit of counsel and might, the spirit of knowledge and of the fear of the Lord. And shall make him of quick understanding . . . and he shall not judge after the sight of his eyes, neither reprove after the hearing of his ears: but with righteousness shall he judge the poor, and reprove with equity for the meek of the earth: and he shall smite the earth with the rod of his mouth, and with the breath of his lips shall he slay the wicked (Isa. 11:1-4).

On the one hand it will be a condition of tranquillity, blessedness, and peace; on the other hand it is instant destruction of the insubordinate, or rebellious. We are living in a time when God is forbearing with wicked men; it is the time of His patience. The Millennium is the "kingdom and the power of the Lord Jesus Christ," and

whatever wickedness shows itself is instantly judged.
Even the nature of the animal kingdom is to be changed.

> The wolf also shall dwell with the lamb, and the
> leopard shall lie down with the kid; and the calf and the
> young lion and the fatling together; and a little child
> shall lead them.

There was no ferocity among the beasts in the Garden
of Eden. Ferocity has come in with the Fall; all creation
fell with man (Rom. 8). We learn also in Romans 8 that
even nature will be delivered from its bondage, or corruption, so as to share the glorious liberty of the children
of God.

> And the cow and the bear shall feed; their young ones
> shall lie down together: and the lion shall eat straw like
> the ox. And the sucking child shall play on the hole of
> the asp, and the weaned child shall put his hand on the
> cockatrice' den. They shall not hurt nor destroy in all
> my holy mountain: for the earth shall be full of the
> knowledge of the Lord, as the waters cover the sea
> (Isa. 11:7-9).

Is that not beautiful?

> And in that day there shall be a root of Jesse, which
> shall stand for an ensign of the people; to it shall the
> Gentiles seek: and his rest shall be glorious (Isa. 11:10).

That is just one of the prophetic pictures of the condition of things during the Millennium. Of this age of
blessedness the prophets give picture after picture. Let
us turn to Romans 8:19-21.

> For the earnest expectation of the creature [creation]
> waiteth for the manifestation of the sons of God. For the
> creature was made subject to vanity, not willingly, but
> by reason of him who hath subjected the same in hope.
> Because the creature itself also shall be delivered from

the bondage of corruption into the glorious liberty of the children of God.

Creation delivered! Creation set free! All the forces about us, the mighty energies of nature, are to be put to the service of man.

What will be the manner of worship on the millennial earth? Ezekiel describes to us not only the distribution of the Holy Land to the tribes of Israel but also the erection of the magnificent millennial temple. There are to be offerings, memorial sacrifices, not expiatory sacrifices. Zechariah adds another significant truth with regard to the Gentile nations:

> And it shall come to pass, that every one that is left of all the nations which came against Jerusalem shall even go up from year to year to worship the King, the Lord of hosts, and to keep the feast of tabernacles (Zech. 14:16).

Pilgrimages from all the nations of the earth will wend their way annually to that most magnificent city, as it will then be the center of the millennial earth's splendor, civilization, and worship. Every eye will be directed there to the worship of the King, the Lord of hosts.

What is to be the end of all this? Alas, dear friend, one shrinks from opening that page; but it must be. Will it always be true that man, tried in every way, is a failure? It has been true, has it not? Man, put in the Garden of Eden, in a paradise where every wish was anticipated, disobeyed the only command that God gave him; and his life there closed in judgment; he was expelled. That man's descendants became so wicked that it was mercy to blot them out by the great judgment of the Flood.

Again there was the dispersion caused by the confusion of tongues at Babel. Was it not judgment that sent them forth as wanderers over the whole earth? Then the Lord finally sent His Son—perfect loveliness—into the world. He was spiked to a cross, the deathbed for the Son of God. The picture which the prophets give to the close of this present age repeats the same story of apostasy.

> And when the thousand years are expired, Satan shall be loosed out of his prison, and shall go out to deceive the nations which are in the four quarters of the earth, Gog and Magog, to gather them together to battle: the number of whom is as the sand of the sea (Rev. 20:7, 8).

No sooner is Satan loosed than he finds a vast multitude ready, as now, to obey him and to believe his lie rather than God's truth. After a thousand years of the manifestation of perfect righteousness, perfect peace, and perfect blessing on the earth, there is still latent in the human heart that pride which is ready to become insubordinate to so gentle a ruler as Jesus.

> And they went up on the breadth of the earth, and compassed the camp of the saints about, and the beloved city: and fire came down from God out of heaven, and devoured them (Rev. 20:9).

That is the last of the earth judgments.

> And the devil that deceived them was cast into the lake of fire and brimstone, where the beast and the false prophet are, and shall be tormented day and night for ever and ever. And I saw a great white throne, and him that sat on it, from whose face the earth and the heaven fled away; and there was found no place for them (Rev. 20:10, 11).

This is not the judgment of the living nations, which takes place when the Lord comes. That is to have taken place on earth; this judgment will be in space.

> And I saw the dead, small and great, stand before

God; and the books were opened: and another book was opened, which is the book of life: and the dead were judged out of those things which were written in the books, according to their works . . . And death and hell were cast into the lake of fire. This is the second death (Rev. 20:12, 14).

Then what?

And I saw a new heaven and a new earth: for the first heaven and the first earth were passed away (Rev. 21:1).

The long, strange, tragic drama of earth has ended. Eternity has begun.

(Used by permission of Arno C. Gaebelein, Inc., publishers of *Our Hope*)

DOOMSDAY

Theodore H. Epp

DOOMSDAY is a word which is very commonly, yet very thoughtlessly used. Often it is employed to designate unlimited time. It is very possible that Satan may have something to do with the common use of this word, for certainly he would like to have people remain unconscious of the certainty of the judgment that is not too far in the future. One can clearly see, then, that if Satan inspires the careless use of such a word in our everyday language, soon men will become unconscious of the reality of coming judgment.

But the fact remains that judgment is sure for the unsaved and that it cannot be far in the future. "And as it is appointed unto men once to die, but after this the judgment" (Heb. 9:27). The final judgment for the unsaved is described in Revelation 20:11-15.

> And I saw a great white throne, and him that sat on it, from whose face the earth and the heaven fled away; and there was found no place for them. And I saw the dead, small and great, stand before God; and the books were opened: and another book was opened, which is the book of life: and the dead were judged out of those things which were written in the books, according to their works. And the sea gave up the dead which were in it; and death and hell delivered up the dead which were in them: and they were judged every man according to their works. And death and hell were cast into the lake of fire. This is the second death. And whosoever

was not found written in the book of life was cast into
the lake of fire.

In fundamental as well as modernistic circles much
teaching has been set forth to make people believe that
there is to be only one great general judgment, at which
time all men will stand before Christ and will be separated as the sheep are from the goats. Much of this false
interpretation of God's judgment plans is based upon a
complete misunderstanding of Matthew 25:31-46. It is
necessary that we read this passage with care and note
that it does not mean a general judgment of all people.
The Scriptures plainly teach that the basis for separating
true believers from unbelievers will be the blood of Jesus
Christ and that men will be judged according to the Gospel. Matthew 25:31-46 does not mention the blood and
atonement at all. Therefore, it does not refer to a judgment which separates sinner from saint.

It is well to understand that there are several great
judgments—seven of which we shall enumerate.

1. Man was first judged and sent out of the Garden of
Eden because of failure and sin. Today we are still reap-
ing the results of this judgment. The record is found in
Genesis 3:14-24.

2. The most important judgment preceding the one recorded in Revelation 20 is that of the judgment of sin upon Calvary. It was here that God, having placed sin upon
Christ, judged Him for our sins.

> For even hereunto were ye called: because Christ also
> suffered for us, leaving us an example, that ye should
> follow his steps: who did no sin, neither was guile found
> in his mouth: who, when he was reviled, reviled not
> again; when he suffered, he threatened not; but commit-
> ted himself to him that judgeth righteously: who his own
> self bare our sins in his own body on the tree, that we,

being dead to sins, should live unto righteousness: by
whose stripes ye were healed (I Peter 2:21-24).

3. Another judgment which is not very well understood
by many is the judgment of the conduct of the believers.
This is known as self-judgment and is described in I Corinthians 11:31-32. "For if we would judge ourselves, we
should not be judged. But when we are judged, we are
chastened of the Lord, that we should not be condemned
with the world."

It is, therefore, important that a man examine himself
and, upon finding sin in his life, confess it to God and
keep communion and fellowship clear. "If we confess our
sins, he is faithful and just to forgive us our sins, and to
cleanse us from all unrighteousness" (I John 1:9).

4. Israel, God's elect, will pass through Great Tribulation, which is a judgment specially designated for them to
bring them, as a nation, back to their God and Father. A
description of this judgment may be found in Ezekiel
20:33-38.

5. The believer will also be judged for his works at
the appearing of the Lord Jesus Christ. "For we must all
appear before the judgment seat of Christ; that every one
may receive the things done in his body, according to that
he hath done, whether it be good or bad" (II Cor. 5:10).
The basis of this judgment is described in I Corinthians
3:10-15:

> According to the grace of God which is given unto me,
> as a wise masterbuilder, I have laid the foundation, and
> another buildeth thereon. But let every man take heed
> how he buildeth thereupon. For other foundation can no
> man lay than that is laid, which is Jesus Christ. Now if
> any man build upon this foundation gold, silver, precious
> stones, wood, hay, stubble; every man's work shall be
> made manifest: for the day shall declare it, because it
> shall be revealed by fire; and the fire shall try every

man's work of what sort it is. If any man's work abide
which he hath built thereupon, he shall receive a reward.
If any man's work shall be burned, he shall suffer loss:
but he himself shall be saved; yet so as by fire.

The believer will not come into the judgment of condemnation, since his judgment for condemnation has been
taken in the person of Jesus Christ, as is mentioned in the
second judgment; but the believer will meet Christ and
will be judged according to his works done in the flesh
during the time of his sojourn on earth as a child of God.

6. Another judgment which is of great importance is
that of the living nations (Gentiles). This is described in
Matthew 25:31-46. At the end of the Tribulation judgment the remaining Gentiles will be called before a special throne on which Jesus will sit upon this earth. They
will be judged on the basis of their treatment of God's
people, Israel. Genesis 12:2, 3 states that God will either
bless or curse the nations, depending upon how they treat
His people, Israel. This will be fulfilled in the judgment
described in Matthew 25.

7. The final judgment is often referred to as the Great
White Throne judgment, or as we have chosen to call it,
doomsday. This is described in Revelation 20:11-15. This
judgment has to do with all who have rejected the Lord
Jesus Christ as Saviour during their lifetime on earth. It
is, therefore, designated as the judgment of the dead.

THE GREAT WHITE THRONE

In the Great White Throne judgment truth and justice
will meet sin and rejection. It is known as GREAT because it is here that the Almighty Power will be seen.
Men have scorned and ridiculed the powers of God, but
at the Great White Throne these powers will be manifest
to those who have rejected Christ during their lifetime. It
will be great because of the vast crowds that will be there.

Possibly at no other place in all time or eternity will such great crowds meet in one place.

First of all, every rejecter of Christ, from the time of Adam until the final person who will have rejected Him during his life on earth, will be there. All the evil angels, including Satan and his hordes, will be present. The angelic hosts will also be present with Christ. Then all the saints who have believed and have become members of the Body of Christ will be with Him. In other words, every creature in Heaven, in earth, and under the earth will be present. Christ himself will be upon the throne.

This judgment is also known as great because of the occasion, for it is here that the eternal consequences will be determined. Eternal separation from God will be the result for all who have rejected His salvation in the days when they lived on earth. Furthermore, this judgment is great because of the dignity of the Judge. He who was despised and rejected will then appear in all the dignity and majesty of the Godhead. Furthermore, it is great because it involves the salvation that has been offered. Never in all the annals of history have we seen such a salvation offered to any man or being as that which was offered by God through His Son Jesus Christ at a cost which we will never understand until we see Him.

It is known as the Great *White* Throne. The word *white* speaks of the holiness and purity of the Judge. There will be no politics or juggling of facts there, for the one and only true, holy, pure One will be the judge. Furthermore, white speaks of righteousness—the righteousness of the judgment—for men will at that time receive that which they have deserved. Their judgment will be absolutely righteous. White also contrasts greatly with the blackness of sin.

It is called the Great White *Throne*. Let us contrast

three of the great thrones that are mentioned in the Scriptures, so that we may distinguish between them.

The Eternal Throne of God. It is from this throne, located in Heaven, that He governs the whole universe.

> And immediately I was in the spirit: and, behold, a throne was set in heaven, and one sat on the throne (Rev. 4:2).
>
> To him that overcometh will I grant to sit with me in my throne, even as I also overcame, and am set down with my Father in his throne (Rev. 3:21).
>
> And there shall be no more curse: but the throne of God and of the Lamb shall be in it; and his servants shall serve him (Rev. 22:3).

The Throne of His Glory. This throne is mentioned in Matthew 25:31 and is a temporary throne which will be located on earth immediately after the Tribulation. It will be the throne upon which Christ will sit to judge the living nations, or Gentiles, just before the kingdom period begins.

The Great White Throne (Rev. 20:11). This is the third and final great throne of a judge. It is a judicial throne; it is temporary and for a very special purpose. It is located neither in Heaven nor on earth, for verse 11 states that both Heaven and earth will flee from the presence of His face. Therefore, it must be located somewhere in the middle of the universe. This is not a throne of His mercy, but a throne of final judgment. Isaiah describes a throne that had an altar beside it, where blood may have been offered for atonement. But there is no altar beside the Great White Throne. Sin will be naked and exposed to all. There will be no blood to plead.

The Judge

And I saw a great white throne, and him that sat on

it, from whose face the earth and the heaven fled away; and there was found no place for them (Rev. 20:11).

Who is this judge from whose face the earth and the Heaven fled away? God reveals that all judgment is placed in the hands of the Son: "For the Father judgeth no man, but hath committed all judgment unto the Son" (John 5:22). "And he commanded us to preach unto the people, and to testify that it is he which was ordained of God to be the Judge of quick and dead" (Acts 10:42).

The once nail-pierced hands will here carry the scepter of authority; and the once thorn-crowned head will carry the crown of glory, majesty, and power. The One whose face was described as so marred that men fled from Him will now outshine the sun, and the atmospheric heavens and the earth will flee from His presence.

A further description may be found in II Peter 3:10:

> But the day of the Lord will come as a thief in the night; in the which the heavens shall pass away with a great noise, and the elements shall melt with fervent heat, the earth also and the works that are therein shall be burned up.

He who once was the Saviour has now become the Judge. This was foretold in Philippians 2:6-11.

> Who, being in the form of God, thought it not robbery to be equal with God: but made himself of no reputation, and took upon him the form of a servant, and was made in the likeness of men: and being found in fashion as a man, he humbled himself, and became obedient unto death, even the death of the cross. Wherefore God also hath highly exalted him, and given him a name which is above every name: that at the name of Jesus every knee should bow, of things in heaven, and things in earth, and things under the earth; and that every tongue should confess that Jesus Christ is Lord, to the glory of God the Father.

He who so loved the world that He gave His only be-gotten Son will exercise His wrath because of the love that has been spurned. "He that believeth on the Son hath everlasting life: and he that believeth not the Son shall not see life; but the wrath of God abideth on him" (John 3:36).

Daniel gives us another picture of this great Judge and His throne:

> I beheld till the thrones were cast down, and the Ancient of days did sit, whose garment was white as snow, and the hair of his head like the pure wool: his throne was like the fiery flame, and his wheels as burning fire. A fiery stream issued and came forth from before him: thousand thousands ministered unto him, and ten thousand times ten thousand stood before him: the judgment was set, and the books were opened (Dan. 7:9, 10).

We also find that the angelic hosts and the saints will be accompanying the Lord Jesus Christ at this great judgment. A further word concering these may be found in I Corinthians 6:2, 3:

> Do ye not know that the saints shall judge the world? and if the world shall be judged by you, are ye unworthy to judge the smallest matters? Know ye not that we shall judge angels? how much more things that pertain to this life?

The Judged

"And I saw the dead" (Rev. 20:12). The Scriptures reveal that there art three different kinds of death: physical death, which is cessation of life in this body; spiritual death, which is the absence of the life of God in man; and the second death, which is the eternal, everlasting separation of man (body and soul) from God. The dead spoken of in this passage before us are the spiritually dead, who were dead in their trespasses and sins and who remained dead because they had not received the life that was offered them; therefore, they are the ones to be judged and condemned to a second death.

There will be "small and great" sinners. All ranks of unsaved people—the high and the low, the respected, the outcast, the young, and the old—will stand face to face with Him whom they have rejected. There will be no hiding place. No caves or mountains will cover them or their sins from Him who will come to judge. This judgment will be in mid-air, and all of the unsaved ones will stand beore Him in special, resurrected bodies given to them for this particular occasion. They will be raised unto everlasting shame, according to Daniel—a shame which is now lacking—for sin will then be most prominent. In most circles today, unless men fall into gross sin, the average sin is passed off without any shame. But there will be plenty of shame at that time. It will be a resurrection unto damnation, for the wrath of God will abide on them forever.

We note how carefully God designates the places from which these dead come. Revelation 20:13: "And the sea gave up the dead which were in it; and death and hell delivered up the dead which were in them." The body and the soul of the unsaved will be reunited for this great judgment. The bodies may come forth either from the sea, where many bodies are buried today, or from the graves. The word traslated "death," referred to in this passage, speaks of the graves, or the dust of the earth. From the ashes the bodies will come forth. The word translated "hell" in verse 13 is taken from the Greek word *hades*, which means "the abiding place of the soul of the dead." The souls will come forth from Hades, whereas the bodies will come forth from either the sea or the grave or wherever they may have been laid or destroyed.

THE JUDGMENT

According to this passage in Revelation 20:12, the books will be opened. God has kept a perfect record of all acts, deeds, opportunities and privileges rejected, etc. He does not need the books for Himself, for He never forgets; but He needs them as proof to the individual who will stand before Him. The books will be opened and, no doubt, man's understanding will be such that he will remember that what is recorded in the book is absolutely true. He will be without excuse.

He will be startled, of course, to find that sinful thoughts, words, and deeds committed in secret will suddenly come out into the open. In Numbers 32:23 we read: "Be sure your sin will find you out." Men would love to hide all of their deeds in darkness, but the darkness is light to God. It hides absolutely nothing.

Proverbs 28:13 says: "He that covereth his sins shall not prosper: but whoso confesseth and forsaketh them shall have mercy." Nothing can be covered before Him, for in that day the sins of the mind will also be exposed. Men may have considered themselves to be sinless, or nearly so; yet we are told in I John 3:15 that "whosoever hateth his brother is a murderer." If there has been hate and malice in a man's heart toward a brother, God will have recorded it in the books and established that he is a murderer.

We look with horror upon the sin of adultery, yet very few will find themselves to be free from that sin. Matthew 5:27, 28 makes it very plain that "whosoever looketh on a woman to lust after her hath committed adultery with her already in his heart." It is, therefore, not only the act of sin that will be judged in that day but also the sins of the heart. No one will be able to stand against the sure record of God.

Paul says that judgment will also be according to his Gospel (Rom. 2:16). "In the day when God shall judge the secrets of men by Jesus Christ according to my gospel." John 3:18 says that "he that believeth not is condemned already." The Gospel is simply the good news that there is salvation in Christ Jesus—sin having been put away through His death. By His resurrection He is able to justify us and become our life. "He that hath the Son hath life, and he that hath not the Son of God hath not life." Actually the judgment will center around the fact that men who stand in this judgment to be judged are the ones who have rejected the offer of salvation. According to the privilege, opportunity, and knowledge that they have had, they will be judged. Men who have attempted to cleanse their own lives and by a moral life attain eternal life will find themselves judged. First John 1:7 tells us that the blood of Jesus Christ "cleanseth us from all sin," and Hebrews 9:22 says that without the shedding of blood there is no remission of sin.

Some of the details of the judgment are left out, but we have indications that there will be degrees of judgment based upon the knowledge and the opportunity that the persons have had and have rejected. Several passages of Scripture indicate this very plainly. Read carefully Romans 2:11-14:

> For there is no respect of persons with God. For as many as have sinned without law shall also perish without law: and as many as have sinned in the law shall be judged by the law; (for not the hearers of the law are just before God, but the doers of the law shall be justified. For when the Gentiles, which have not the law, do by nature the things contained in the law, these, having not the law, are a law unto themselves.)

The indication is very clear here that all who have rejected Christ will pass into eternal death, or separation

from God. In some way or another God will mete out
righteous judgment. This will not be in terms of years, for
we are told that the judgment is eternal. This is plainly
indicated in Matthew 11:22-24.

> But I say unto you, It shall be more tolerable for
> Tyre and Sidon at the day of judgment, than for you.
> And thou, Capernaum, which art exalted unto heaven,
> shalt be brought down to hell: for if the mighty works,
> which have been done in thee, had been done in Sodom,
> it would have remained until this day. But I say unto
> you, That it shall be more tolerable for the land of Sodom
> in the day of judgment, than for thee.

In Luke 12:47, 48 we find this: "And that servant, which
knew his Lord's will, and prepared not himself, neither
did according to his will, shall be beaten with many
stripes. But he that knew not, and did commit things wor-
thy of stripes, shall be beaten with few stripes." What is
meant by this degree of judgment, we are not told in the
Scriptures. The only thing of which we can definitely be
sure is that a righteous God will deal righteously and
justly with all sin. That the judgment is eternal we
have already seen and established. Chapter 20 of Revelation makes this very plain. How the degrees of judgment
will be meted out can be known only in the future.

This judgment is known to end in the second death.
The second death is the eternal, everlasting separation of
man from God. Man will be cast into a literal, burning Hell, where he must remain for eternity, never again
to have the privilege of seeing God or knowing His wonderful mercies. "And death and hell were cast into the
lake of fire. This is the second death. And whosoever was
not found written in the book of life was cast into the lake
of fire" (Rev. 20:14, 15).

How can we escape this judgment? First, we must be
identified with Christ, for Christ is this eternal life. "He

that hath the Son hath life; and he that hath not the Son of God hath not life." We are given the privilege of becoming the children of God by receiving Christ (John 1:12). "But as many as received him, to them gave he power to become the sons of God, even to them that believe on his name." By being identified with Him, and having accepted Him, we receive everlasting life. "Jesus said unto her, I am the resurrection, and the life: he that believeth in me, though he were dead, yet shall he live: and whosoever liveth and believeth in me shall never die. Believest thou this?" (John 11:25, 26). Man's basis for this eternal life is faith, for Christ says plainly, "Believest thou this?"

Only in this life do we have the opportunity of receiving Christ and becoming the sons of God. "He, that being often reproved hardeneth his neck, shall suddenly be destroyed, and that without remedy" (Prov. 29:1). "How shall we escape, if we neglect so great salvation?" (Heb. 2:3).

There will be no opportunity for a person to accept Christ after this life. It is now or never! If you are not a child of God, accept Him as your Saviour today.

THE FUTURE STATE

C. I. Scofield

W E SHALL NOW LOOK at what lies beyond time, in eternity. Only revelation can speak here. Of that which is past, history may tell a broken and imperfect story. Of that which lies in the immediate future, the signs of the times may give us some premonition; but when we seek to pass beyond time and beyond signs, when we would know the eternal state, we can know only what God has revealed.

Science cannot help us. Scientists tell us that it is unscientific and irrational to infer that physical death is the cessation of all life. We see that other forces survive changes of form, and it is not according to analogy to say that the force which we call life, which has its manifestation for a few years in the mortal body, ceases with the change which we call death. That is the message of science. How unsatisfactory it is, after all! If we die we shall live again! But how shall we live, and where shall we live? Do our choices here affect our destiny there? These are the questions that spring to the lips and demand an answer; and these questions are not merely speculative; they have the most direct bearing upon character and conduct.

"If a man die, shall he live again?" There is something within us that craves completeness. We do not go very far in this life before we find that incompleteness marks even the most fortunate human life. In each life we find defeated aspiration, imperfect achievement, and the soul's reaching out for things which the hand cannot grasp. So

113

we ask, "Is there another sphere beyond, where the incompleteness of this life may find fullness?"

We follow our beloved dead to the grave. As we lay away all that is tangible and visible of them, we ask over each newly made mound, "If a man die, shall he live again?" The affection which we believe to be of God reaches out empty arms into the beyond. Love leaps over the little trench which we call a grave, and we stand there asking, "Is there life beyond? Is this the end, or may we presently take up the interrupted fellowship in some happier sphere?"

There is another question which demands an answer: Is this present life determinative of the life beyond? If this life is determinative of the life beyond, the eternal state is the greatest of all influences in the formation of character and the determination of conduct. If we believe this, everything begins to take color from it. I repeat that the questions we ask concerning the hereafter are not speculative questions.

Is there an answer? If we turn to Scripture, we shall find an answer, not an answer which meets every idle, curious surmise, but an answer which, if received, satisfies every legitimate question of the soul. As far as I know, not one who has come with a serious purpose to seek the Bible's answer to the questions concerning the hereafter has ever complained of its inadequacy.

It is true that "it doth not yet appear what we shall be." Innumerable questions might be asked concerning the future of saint or sinner which are not answered in Scripture. But, on the other hand, enough is told to give rest to the mind. "We know," said John, "that, when he shall appear, we shall be like him." That is Heaven anywhere—to be with Christ and like Him. In considering what is revealed concerning the hereafter, we shall find that the

message of the Bible lies partly in its doctrinal statements
and partly in its prophetical unfoldings.

Here the very volume of truth compels me to summarize. It would be impossible, even within a very liberal
limit of time, to present to you in detail all the testimony
of Scripture concerning the future state. I shall, therefore,
summarize it in a series of propositions, reading from the
Scripture which establishes the truth of these propositions.

DEATH IS NOT THE END

The first of these summary propositions is this: Death
is the cessation neither of existence nor of consciousness.

The first answer which Scripture makes to the question
as to what lies beyond death is that physical death, the
death of the body, is not the end of life or of consciousness; that is, there is something which lives after the body
dies, and that something is in full possession of consciousness. In proof of this I shall quote, first of all, the words of
the Lord Jesus Christ in Luke 16. With His own hand He
lifts the veil here and permits us to see what occurs beyond death, both to one who died unreconciled to God
and to one who was His child.

> There was a certain rich man, which was clothed in
> purple and fine linen, and fared sumptuously every day:
> and there was a certain beggar named Lazarus, which
> was laid at his gate, full of sores, and desiring to be fed
> with crumbs which fell from the rich man's table: more-
> over the dogs came and licked his sores. And it came to
> pass that the beggar died, and was carried by the angels
> into Abraham's bosom: the rich man also died, and was
> buried; and in hell [hades] he lift up his eyes, being in
> torments, and seeth Abraham afar off, and Lazarus in
> his bosom.

Perhaps you are saying, "Yes, but this is a parable." In
the first place, I do not know of anything which authorizes

you to call it a parable. There have been many rich men
and many beggars on the earth; and I do not think that the
Lord Jesus Christ had to invent a rich man or a beggar.
Many beggars have also been full of sores at the gates of
rich men. But granting that we have a parable here, the
Lord Jesus Christ is surely incapable of teaching error,
either by the statement of a fact or by a method of teaching called the parable. In either case the teaching is the
principal thing, and in either case the teaching is true because Jesus Christ said it.

"The beggar died." Well, beggars die now. The death of
a beggar is not an uncommon phenomenon on this earth.
Rich men also die. Death is the common fate of all man-
kind. There is nothing remarkable about it. But what
happened to the beggar after he died?

> And it came to pass, that the beggar died, and was
> carried by the angels into Abraham's bosom: the rich
> man also died, and was buried; and in hell [hades] he
> lift up his eyes, being in torments.

As we read on, we see that the man in Hades is very
much alive; he carries on conversations; he has a memory;
he remembers that he has relatives still living on the earth
who may come to that place; and he desires that someone
be sent back to the earth to warn them.

Bear in mind that I quote this passage at this time simply to support the first proposition, that death is the cessation neither of existence nor of consciousness. The beggar and the rich man are both alive and conscious after
death. We turn now to Revelation 6:9:

> And when he had opened the fifth seal, I saw under
> the altar the souls of them that were slain for the word of
> God, and for the testimony which they held: and they
> cried with a loud voice, saying, How long, O Lord, holy
> and true, dost thou not judge and avenge our blood on

them that dwell on the earth? And white robes were
given unto every one of them; and it was said unto
them, that they should rest yet for a little season.

These souls under the altar are living; they are very
conscious of where they came from and of what is to occur
on the earth. They are thoroughly alive and thoroughly
conscious.

SEPARATION AT DEATH

Second proposition: Death is eternal separation of the
saved and the unsaved. Read further from Luke 16. Notice especially verse 26:

And beside all this, between us and you there is a
great gulf fixed: so that they which would pass from
hence to you cannot; neither can they pass to us, that
would come from thence.

Read also Matthew 25:46:

"And these shall go away into everlasting punishment:
but the righteous into life eternal."

The words *eternal* and *everlasting* are translated from
the same word in the original, a word which expresses the
duration of separation. In Revelation 21:1-8 we read that
the eternal abode of the saved is the heavenly Jerusalem,
and the eternal abode of the lost is the lake of fire.

The condition beyond death involves, first, conscious
existence and, second, the eternal separation of the saved
and the lost. In this world the good and the bad are mingled together. The wicked do not cease from causing
trouble here, and the weary do not here find rest; but this
mixed condition does not continue in the next world. The
rule hereafter is separation—separation of the saved from
the unsaved.

Abode of the Dead

Third proposition: From the moment of death the saved are with the Lord, and the unsaved are in Hades awaiting the judgment.

Let us read again from Luke 16, the great foundation passage of all this line of truth:

> And it came to pass, that the beggar died, and was carried by the angels into Abraham's bosom: the rich man also died . . . And in hell [hades] he lift up his eyes, being in torments.

From this we see that the lost soul goes immediately into Hades. We shall see later what becomes of those who are in Hades. In II Corinthians 5:6-8 we find:

> Therefore we are always confident, knowing that, whilst we are at home in the body, we are absent from the Lord: (for we walk by faith, not by sight:) we are confident, I say, and willing rather to be absent from the body, and to be present with the Lord.

There are two places, so to speak, for the saved man. He may be living in the body; and so far as the personal presence of the Lord is concerned, he would be "absent from the Lord." Or he may be absent from the body and personally present with the Lord. But there is no intermediate place, or waiting place. A Christian is either in the body and not in the personal presence of the Lord (of course, he is always under His loving eye and in His mighty hand), or he is absent from the body and present with the Lord. He does not yet have his resurrection body; but he is "present with the Lord." Read II Peter 2:9:

> The Lord knoweth how to deliver the godly out of temptations, and to reserve the unjust unto the day of judgment to be punished.

The lost are not immediately judged, but they are re-

served "unto the day of judgment to be punished." There
is no other possible prospect before a lost soul. That place
of detention, as we know from many passages, is called
"hades" and is to be distinguished from the "lake of fire,"
which is the place of final punishment of the unsaved.

THE FUTURE FOR THE SAVED

Fourth proposition: At the second coming of Christ the
saved receive their resurrection bodies and enter upon
their eternal activities.

The state of the saved between death and resurrection
is always said in Scripture to be one of rest. It is not un-
consciousness, but rest. The souls under the altar cry,
"How long?" They are told to rest a little while. Glorious
activities await the redeemed in eternity, but they are
not entered upon until the resurrection has reunited spirit,
soul, and body. This occurs at the second coming of
Christ. Let us turn now to I Corinthians 15:22, 23.

> For as in Adam all die, even so in Christ shall all be
> made alive. But every man in his own order: Christ the
> firstfruits; afterwards they that are Christ's at his coming.

I do not know how there has crept into the thought of
man and somewhat into the books that men write the
idea of a simultaneous resurrection of the just and the
unjust. The Scriptures never speak of one simultaneous,
universal resurrection. It is expressly stated that "all
that are in the graves shall hear his voice, and shall come
forth" (John 5:28, 29). But two resurrections are immediately described. Turn now to I Thessalonians 4:15-
17:

> For this we say unto you by the word of the Lord, that
> we which are alive and remain unto the coming of the
> Lord shall not prevent them which are asleep. For the
> Lord himself shall descend from heaven with a shout,

with the voice of the archangel, and with the trump of God: and the dead in Christ shall rise first: then we which are alive and remain shall be caught up together with them in the clouds, to meet the Lord in the air: and so shall we ever be with the Lord.

When Christ descends from Heaven with a shout, with the voice of the archangel, and with the trump of God at His second coming, the dead in Christ will be raised.

For our conversation [citizenship] is in heaven; from whence also we look for the Saviour, the Lord Jesus Christ: who shall change our vile body, that it may be fashioned like unto his glorious body, according to the working whereby he is able even to subdue all things unto himself (Phil. 3:20, 21).

This passage, as you see, completes the teaching of the Thessalonian passage. The Christian dead are raised; the living Christians are changed physically into the likeness of the resurrection body of Jesus. Both classes, living believers and believers whose bodies are in the graves at the second advent of Christ, are in view in the well-known passage in I Corinthians 15:51, 52:

Behold, I show you a mystery; we shall not all sleep, but we shall all be changed, in a moment, in the twinkling of an eye, at the last trump: for the trumpet shall sound, and the dead shall be raised incorruptible, and we shall be changed.

Read also Revelation 20:4-6:

And I saw thrones, and they sat upon them, and judgment was given unto them: and I saw the souls of them that were beheaded for the witness of Jesus, and for the word of God, and which had not worshiped the beast, neither his image, neither had received his mark upon their foreheads, or in their hands; and they lived and reigned with Christ a thousand years. But the rest of the dead lived not again until the thousand years were finished. This is the first resurrection. Blessed and holy is he that hath part in the first resurrection: on such the second death hath no power, but they shall be priests of God and of Christ, and shall reign with him a thousand years.

Between the resurrection of those who are Christ's and the resurrection of "the rest of the dead," who are not Christ's, there intervenes one thousand years of time—the millennial period.

THE FATE OF THE WICKED

Fifth proposition: At the end of the Millennium the unsaved receive their resurrected bodies, are judged, and are cast into the lake of fire.

And I saw a great white throne, and him that sat on it, from whose face the earth and the heaven fled away; and there was found no place for them. And I saw the dead, small and great, stand before God (Rev. 20:11, 12).

As we have just seen, those who are Christ's have already been raised from among the dead and have been reigning with Christ for one thousand years. It is after the thousand years are expired that this Great White Throne is set up, and is "the dead" who stand before God.

I once supposed that at some time I would stand in space with the vast throng of all who had ever lived on this earth before that Great White Throne, that the books would be opened, that all my sins would be read out of those books, and that another book would then be opened from which it might appear that I had been saved. If the man by my side had not been saved, he would pass on into the lake of fire; and thus the eternal parting would take place. There is not a line of Scripture which supports this thought. No Christian stands before the Great White Throne. Every Christian is a glorified saint then. The passage cited from Corinthians states clearly that those who are Christ's are raised at His coming, and there are left behind for the second resurrection only the bodies of the lost and the wicked dead.

"I saw the dead, small and great." This was not the living who had been reigning with Christ for one thousand years, His Bride; but it was "the dead." Think of it! You have received your glorious body, have stood before the Judgment Seat of Christ as your works (not sins) passed His scrutiny, have been married to Him, have returned with Him in glory to the earth, and have been enthroned with Him; now are you to descend from that place and stand with the wicked dead who have just been raised from their graves to have it determined whether you are saved or not? The idea, of course, is preposterous! Furthermore, there is not a word of Scripture, or a syllable, which supports it.

But God forbid that we should study this subject in cold blood. Try to think of this scene; try to realize its measureless horror—the dead standing before God! Most of them will, I believe, be speechless; but some will cry out in astonishment. "Lord, Lord, have we not prophesied in thy name and in thy name done many wonderful works?" Poor, deluded professors of religion! They trusted in religion and works rather than in Christ. Now they must hear Him who would have saved them say, "I never knew you." The record, the damning record, will be there in case any soul thinks to cry out against the justice of God in that awful scene. I, for one, can never read Revelation 20 without yearning over every soul that is putting off the question of salvation and staying outside of Christ. You and I may have our names written in the Book of

Life. Oh, marvel of grace! Think of it! Is your name written there? That is the important question. Is it there?

Then we learn the result of this judgment.

> And death and hell [hades] [the contents of them] were cast into the lake of fire. This is the second death (Rev. 20:14).

HEAVEN

Two questions now remain. (1) What is Heaven, and why are the saved so happy there? (2) What is this lake of fire, or "Gehenna," as it is elsewhere called, and why are the lost so wretched there? Let us look at these questions briefly in the light of Scripture.

First of all, Heaven is a place. Get that very clearly in your mind. I used to think of it as a state of being, a disembodied condition (perhaps here on earth). As a little boy I shuddered and shrank from becoming a ghost, and I thought how cold, bleak, and uncomfortable it must be! When I confided all this to someone, I was told that I would be an angel if I were good; and I would have wings and a harp. Let us get these unscriptural notions out of our minds. Heaven is a place, a "prepared" place, which means a suited place.

> Let not your heart be troubled: ye believe in God, believe also in me. In my Father's house are many mansions: if it were not so, I would have told you. I go to prepare a place for you (John 14:1, 2).

These words can convey to our minds only ideas of locality and substantial entity. We know this at least— Heaven is; spiritualize it as you please. On the other hand, we are not to suppose that Heaven is a place full of brown stone houses. That would be a very crude and fleshly conception of it. I do not know what glorified architecture is

like; but I do know that the Christ who has sown this
earth with flowers, lifted it into majestic mountains, set
the continents in the tossing seas, and filled the upper air
with drifting clouds and azure depths is the same Christ
whose hand is shaping the eternal love-home for His
Bride. "I go to prepare a place for you." That is enough
for me.

Turn with me now to Revelation 21:1:

> And I saw a new heaven and a new earth: for the first
> heaven and the first earth were passed away; and there
> was no more sea.

There was no end after all, but continuity, change,
development—a new Heaven and a new earth.

The chief conditions of happiness in this prepared
place, according to Scripture, are two; but the co-operant
conditions are almost innumerable. I am perfectly willing
to state one of them in the exact language of science.
Herbert Spencer, the agnostic scientist, was asked what,
from the scientific standpoint, would be required to make
a Heaven. His answer was this: "A perfect being in a
perfect environment." I am willing to give you that, the
language of an agnostic, as the expression of what Scripture has to say about happiness in Heaven.

In Heaven our bodies will be perfected into the image
of Jesus Christ (Phil. 3:21; I John 3:2). Every trace of
sin, infirmity, weakness, and imperfection will be left behind; and we shall be changed into the glorious fullness
of the image of Jesus Christ.

Then these perfected beings will be in a perfected environment. There will be no taint of sin there, no death,
no grave, no separation, and no growing old and infirm.
All of these things will be banished forever.

The other condition of the blessedness of the saint
might be called a negative one; it is the absence of the

things which make misery here. We read that "God shall
wipe away all tears from their eyes; and there shall be
no more death." However perfectly we might arrange an
Eden here or however heavenly we might make some
small portion of earth, we know that the stealthy tread
of death will come there. Would it be Heaven where
death exists? I do not want any such Heaven. I want to go
to a better Heaven than that.

> There shall be no more death, neither sorrow, nor
> crying, neither shall there be any more pain [mental pain
> or physical pain]: for the former things are passed away.

HELL

What is the lake of fire, where the lost are, and why
are they wretched there?

First of all, the lake of fire is a place, just as Heaven is
a place. Let us read Matthew 25:41:

> Then shall he say also unto them on the left hand, De-
> part from me, ye cursed, into everlasting fire, prepared
> for the devil and his angels.

Men tell me sometimes that they would find it very
difficult to believe in a God who had prepared such a
place as the lake of fire for His creatures. He never did
it! He prepared that awful place "for the devil and his
angels." If you go there, you will go there against the
pleading of God. You will go past the cross to get there;
you will go there over the dead body of God's Son. You
will go there because you resolve to go there. You will
go there in spite of the fact that God has already paid
the price of your redemption in the blood of His Son
and made a way of escape for you. He has taken away all
the barriers that His holiness and justice might have inter-
posed between you and Heaven. He has swung wide the

doors and said that whosoever will may come. He warns you that He has prepared a place for the Devil and his angels, and He implores you to be saved from it.

You do not have to do anything bad to go there—just keep on neglecting to be saved.

If anyone goes there, he will find conditions of wretchedness. He will be eternally separated from God and righteousness.

What does that mean? Do not people get on fairly well without God here? My friend, you do not get on without God a fleeting second of your life. If God were to withhold His mercies from the most wicked man who walks this earth, he would fall into unspeakable torment at once. Every day God showers mercies upon the very men who will not have Him, those who will not believe on His Son. The vilest wretch, the coldest atheist, or the most immaculate moralist alive on this earth is not without God or separate from Him. God is filling his life with blessings every day, every one of which is designed to melt his heart and turn him to Jesus.

Many a man outside of Christ would not want his wife to be unsaved for anything in the world. He would not have his children without Christian training. I am glad of that—but think of it!

In Hades first and afterward in the lake of fire there is eternal separation from God and righteousness. It means absolute hopelessness. The most wretched man who lives on this earth has some lingering ray of hope in his heart, but the soul in Hell hopes for nothing. His heart is fixed in desperate hatred of God; his unchanged character is fixed in love of evil. Look at the character of the rich man of Luke 16 in Hades. What does he want? He wants Lazarus, the poor beggar whose life was filled with disease and suffering, sent down into his place of torment so that he may be comforted a little. He is the same swine

of selfishness that he was on earth; and it is Hell enough
to carry that kind of a character throughout eternity.
When he realizes that he cannot get Lazarus down there
with him so that, at whatever cost to Lazarus, his tongue
may be cooled, he wants poor Lazarus sent back to the
earth so that a miracle may be wrought in behalf of his
wicked brothers who have already heard the Word of
God without heeding its warnings. Think of the hellish
selfishness of those two requests. There will be no man
in Hell who would not tear God from His throne if he
could. The black natural heart is there.

Scripture makes it very clear that the natural emotions
are there. Judas hanged himself in remorse. Do you suppose that the remorse stopped when his life went out
through the tightened noose about his neck? His remorse
is yet gnawing at his heart. The man in Hades remem-
bered. He sat there in torment with memory and with
consciousness. "Son, remember," said Abraham. Oh, if
they could forget! What would they give if they could
forget? But there is no forgetting. "Son, remember." Remember God's offer of mercy repeated again and again.
Are you going to sit in Hades sometime and remember
that God offered to save you, that it cost Him the blood
of His Son to be able righteously to make that offer, and
that you said, "I will put it off a little longer"?

The rich man said, "Father Abraham, I have five
brothers." Probably he was the eldest of them, and he
had lived the wrong kind of life before them. They were
on their way to Hell, and he had had a good deal to do
with it. Think of the brothers in torment saying, "You did
it; you asked me to take my first drink; you led me into my
first sin; you were older than I, and I thought that I could
do it. I saw you going into barrooms and other places
worse than that; I thought it was smart and manly, and
I went in also."

Oh, turn ye, turn ye, my unbelieving friend! Why will ye die? These things are awful realities. What is the great shining message that God sends out of Heaven? Listen! "For God so loved the world, that he gave his only begotten Son, that whosoever believeth in him should not perish, but have everlasting life." Will you have it now? Are you saying, "Well, what must I do"? I shall tell you what to do. Bow your head just now, and let these words be yours.

"Lord Jesus, I have sinned; I have done evil. Thou hast died for me. I take Thee for my Saviour. I trust Thee; I put my soul into Thy care. I give myself to Thee to be cleansed of sin and to be saved for eternity. Amen."

(Reprinted from *Addresses on Prophecy*, used by permission of Arno C. Gaebelein, Inc., publishers of *Our Hope*)